ACT LIKE A LADY
THINK LIKE A
QUEEN

J.B. ALLEN

Copyright 2021
Jennifer B. Allen

Printed in the United States of America

Library of Congress-Catalogued in Publication Data

ISBN 13: 978-1-7339678-4-6(Paperback)

Reflection Photography and Publishing LLC.
www.jenniferballen.com

Many of the personal stories and testimonies included in this book were provided with permission to the author through a series of personal interviews conducted during the writing of the original version of this book. For all other stories, names and identifying details have been changed.

Cover design by Augusto Silva-acesosilva@gmail.com

Table of Contents

Acknowledgments

I would like to thank all those who have always believed in me and encouraged me to be my best. I truly appreciate the level of accountability you all hold me to. It encourages me to keep pushing.

To my husband, my biggest cheerleader, thank you honey for allowing me to walk in my truth and fulfilling the call on my life. I know you may get tired of my demanding schedule at times, but I thank you for always being willing and able to be by my side wherever I go. I love you.

Thanks to my children who are truly my heartbeats. You guys make me feel like a virtuous woman. This book is dedicated to you ladies. I pray you find some value in it. I am so proud of each of you. You too are virtuous. I love you.

To my overseer, mentors, family, and friends, all I can say is thank you. I thank God for each of you being in my life. I am truly blessed.

Introduction

Queens, it seems, since feminism has become a part of our culture we have become extremely intrigued by the mannerisms of our male counterparts. We want to know what makes them tick. When we are attracted to them, we are all trying to figure them out.

Fortunately for us, plenty of books out there talk to us about how a man thinks and what makes them tick. Books that are usually written by other men. I guess that would be the best source when discussing how a man thinks and why he does the things he does.

Usually, the author discloses to us some spicy secrets, breaking all man codes to educate us on how to handle our men and get into their heads.

There are books like "Never Satisfied; How and Why Men Cheat" by Michael Baisden, and Steve Harvey's book "Act Like a Lady, Think Like a Man." Both books became best-sellers, amongst others with similar content, because we women want to know, why and how?

I must admit when both books came out, I was very intrigued to find out what spicy man tips were within the content of the books, and I purchased them both. I also watched, "Act Like a Lady, Think Like a Man", the movie. I liked the book better than the movie.

However, I must admit, I didn't agree with most of the approaches taken when dealing with love relationships between a man and a woman, in either books or movies. Although I didn't agree with some of the content, Steve and I do agree on one thing, we should all "Act Like a Lady." Where Steve and I differ is I believe instead of trying to think like a man, we should turn our focus on becoming the best version of ourselves. I believe trying to think like a man is a big distraction.

I am not sharing my opinion, on this subject, to counter Steve or other men. I am not here to man-bash, either. I am sharing this because we need to have this conversation. When it comes to relationships many of us are just doing it wrong. We are missing the mark. We are either getting into relationships that leave us damaged or leaving relationships while causing damage to others.

I think a lot of the advice we get from our male counterparts is great advice. But what they fail to tell us is all men don't think alike. We cannot put all men in one big bubble or compartmentalize them. They are different. We must deal with everyone accordingly, as we learn them.

I found after I took my focus off them, dealt with them on a case-by-case basis, and focused on me, my relationships with them improved. I began to center my mind on bettering myself.

Becoming the best version of yourself requires a lot of self-examination and self-preservation. Both are important. I've found that as we get closer to becoming whom we were created to be, we will begin to love ourselves differently, in a more powerful way. We become less afraid to look at ourselves in the mirror and hold ourselves accountable and to a higher standard of thinking.

Ladies, it is human nature to want to be loved. In Greek mythology, there are seven types of love. I want to discuss two in this book. The first is Eros love, the sexual and passionate love between a man and a woman. The second is Philautia (Fi-lo-te-a) love, which is the love for self. I believe the latter is the most important one of all.

I am not an expert on how a man thinks, that is not what I will be discussing with you. I am an expert on how a queen should think. This book is about transforming the mindset and ideologies when it comes to dating, marriage, or waiting.

As we are waiting, seeking, finding, or experiencing Eros love, we should experience it by thinking and behaving like a queen as defined in the dictionary. If not, we may be left brokenhearted, damaged, and highly disappointed. At the same time damaging good men.

Queens, we need to learn how to stay in our lane; focusing on things we can change. My mantra is better decisions today, lead to fewer regrets later.

Now I don't expect everyone to agree with me, because my opinion does come from a Christian woman's point of view, so it's ok to agree to disagree. At the end of the day, we all face the same issues as women when dealing with our male counterparts, Christian or not. I think this conversation is way overdue. For those who will accept my point of view let's get real, keep it real, and have this conversation, Queen, to Queen.

Chapter One

A Queen's Behavior

"Queenliness is more than a title. It's a lifestyle"~ J. B. Allen

I hear and see so many women referring to themselves as queens, Queen this and Queen that. I honestly love to see women holding themselves in such high regard.

However, what I have realized over the years is queen status is earned. Being treated like a queen requires us to act like queens.

There are several definitions of a queen, but the one that stands out to me the most is the definition that defines a queen as being a woman or girl, who is "very important" or successful at something. A queen is a woman who is "very important." She is important to God, herself, and others. Now those are some big shoes to fill.

I am under the impression that with that level of affirmation comes a higher level of accountability. As a queen, we can't come up with all types of attitudes and behaviors. When we're trying to identify ourselves as queens, there are some character traits we must possess. We can label ourselves as queens all day. But are we really in queenship defined as "very important" to others outside of ourselves? Ladies we live in a big world. If we are looking for a relationship, we should desire to be "very important" or significant to our mates or our significant other. If not, we will never be able to speak to that king in him. Nor will we be worth it to him to make any adjustments needed to love us the way we desire to be loved.

Even if you have no desire for a relationship, you should still desire to walk in queenship. That status demands a certain level of respect. Respect that starts with self-first. Self-respect exudes from us until everyone else must follow suit.

I want to be clear, queenship behavior is for you, not him. This is about us becoming the best version of ourselves. This is important as we are becoming who were created to be, while we are dealing with our kings. For this reason, we should show up with our mental checklist of what our good fit (man/king) looks like to us. But first, let's talk about a queen's behavior.

First, a queen is wise, and she knows how to speak to her king. Just like in the book of Esther, in the Bible.

According to the Bible, Queen Esther was the queen of Persia. She was an orphan girl raised by a cousin and was taken against her own will and presented to the King of Persia, Ahasuerus (*uh*-haz-yoo-**eer**-*uh* s). Before Esther was queen, the Queen of Persia was Vashti. Vashti was a queen who truly knew herself. She refused to allow even the King to dishonor her in front of his drunken associates. Old Hebrew scriptures described her as vain and wicked. I disagree. Nevertheless, the King couldn't handle it. His Chief Advisors thought Vashti was argumentative, belligerent, and defied the King. They were afraid she was setting a trend by disrespecting her man, and that other women in the kingdom would follow.

The king had been embarrassed or disrespected by Vashti, so he dismissed her. Kicked her to the curb. He sought out a new Queen.

Then came Esther. Queen Esther had to use her position to speak to her King about saving her people from the scheme of Haman, the King's Chief Advisor. The Bible says that Esther planned two visits, to speak to her King. Back then they needed permission to speak with the King, even the Queen. On the first visit, she felt him out and decided that that was not the time to drop her request on him. On the second visit, she went in without permission. She spoke to her King and her request was granted.

I used this example to further explain the behavior of a queen. Vashti was a diva, according to some. Her behavior was unbecoming of a Queen, at least by the King's standards. Esther also violated rules, but because of her attitude and behavior, the rules she violated were overlooked.

The bottom line a queen and a diva are two different things. A queen is defined as an important woman to others. Whereas a diva is defined as being self-important. She is only important to herself. They are also defined as temperamental and difficult to please. Do you see the difference? Now, don't get me wrong I am not knocking a diva's mindset. I see being a diva a little differently than Webster. Nonetheless, that is how Webster sees a diva.

Queens a diva behavior (defined by Webster), will not speak to the heart of most kings. Men are difficult and we will never understand their mindsets. They are fickle creatures and can be very emotional and sensitive. We must use wisdom when dealing and communicating with them, especially if we love them and believe they are worth it. So, wisdom is key!

Now I want to come back to Vashti. To me, Vashti epitomizes a queen who knows her worth. That is essential to queenliness. You see although historians described her as vain and wicked, she refused to be belittled in front of a group of inebriated men and lay down her queenliness even for the king himself. Yes, in those days defying the king was inexcusable, but Vashti didn't care. She believed her self-respect meant more. That is not being a feminist, that is being a Queen.

I would like to add. According to this story in the Bible, Vashti had invited a group of ladies over to the palace to enjoy some lady fun. Across the palace her man was partying with his associates, so she had her own get-together, when the king called her to come parade in front of his comrades in her crown, she believed she had to say, "no", out of obligation to the women that were watching her. She knew the influence she had on those women. She was willing to risk her neck to save her reputation and her unadulterated queenliness. Although Vashti is mentioned very little in the Bible. The story goes on to say that after he began to come down off his drunkenness and his so-called outrage, the king missed Vashti. He began to think about her and probably wanted her back. That's when his homeboys got together and planned to get his mind off her by parading some other pretty young things in front of him. Isn't that typical? Nevertheless, just like the old folks would say, "You may not like me, but you will respect me."

I believe he became a better man, and a good husband to Esther, because of Vashti.

With that being said, let me describe what I believe is queen behavior.

A queen's behavior is not a lifestyle change. It's a compilation of character traits. This behavior consists of being honest and respectfully frank, with us first, then others. Being happy and positive, most days, are also traits of a queen's behavior. Self-disciplined, self-confidence, competent, compassionate, and the ability to keep our emotions in check, are also important character traits of a queen. I want to go on to name a few more. Being respectful, starting with self-respect, self-love, self-assured, un-impressionable, humble, authentic, reliable, loving, and kind are also important traits. It may seem like a long list, but it's not, because many of these things go hand in hand.

Queens wherever you are in this, if you're married, in a relationship, single and ready to mingle, or single and waiting, we should all know how to speak to the heart of a king. Now don't get me wrong I am aware that there are good kings and bad kings. Some kings haven't even discovered the king in themselves. It's difficult to speak to a king who doesn't realize he is a king. So, ladies choose your kings wisely. Kingship comes with its own level of accountability. Right now, I just want to focus on speaking to a good king; one that is worth it.

Transparent moment:

When my husband and I were first married the beginning of our marriage was horrid. We argued all the time. Although he never called me out my name, I called him every name in the book. I would say awful things to him. It always seemed the louder I yelled, the less he listened. The more emotional I acted, the less he paid attention. It used to infuriate me to the point I wanted a divorce. But then something happened. I began to pay less attention to his actions and more attention to mine. I changed how I spoke to him. Not just that. I began to speak to the king in him in different ways. I still communicated with him. I let him know what I needed and wanted in a way that didn't appear I was talking at him, as he'd say, but to him. I made it clear. I had made my mind up that I was not going to lose myself in the relationship anymore. I must admit, I had put a time limit on things because I was going to file for a divorce. But as I continued to speak to the king in him with actions and words he began to change. He began to come to me and apologize for his actions. He began to confess to me areas he could improve. Sometimes unprovoked by me. He would send the "I love you so much," texts throughout the day. Things he hadn't done before.

You see the less I focused on trying to convince him of my worth and began to work on me, the more he noticed me. Now don't get me wrong, we are still working through some things. But we love each other. He loves me and I love him. I am certain if I continue to speak to the king in him and he speaks to the queen in me, we will be just fine.

Another transparent moment:

Way back in the day a time when I was very impressionable and vulnerable; I became involved with a guy who was a little rough around the edges. He and I dated for a few years and gave birth to a baby girl. For years he wanted to make his money in a non-traditional way (*try to read between the lines*). Although I was the total opposite of him, there was nothing, I could do to make him find a regular job and be a real family man or king to me.

After we broke up, he met another woman. He met her while we were together, nevertheless, they got together.

With her, he went to a trade school. He studied and got certified in a trade. He got a regular job that paid well and provided regular insurance for him and his daughter they had together. I questioned myself for a while about that. I was wondering to myself what did she have that I didn't have?

Being transparent I know I was not walking in queenship. My mind needed to be renewed. I didn't love myself enough and I didn't know my worth. I didn't even have an idea what I wanted or deserved in or from a man.

I am not sure if she was walking in queenship or not, but what I know is she was able to speak to the king in him, at that time.

That young lady brought out a side of him I had never seen before. A side of him I didn't even know existed. I'm not sure how they are now or how he is. All I know is at that moment in time she brought out the king and for the first time of knowing him, he seemed proud of himself. You see she was able to speak to something in him that I was not able to reach at the time. Honestly, I am not sure if he even knew a king resided in him.

Now I must admit they hurt me back then, but I am giving her, her props. Besides, I am not that chic who will ever damage another queen's crown, even if she has damaged mine. You see that is what queens do. We look out for one another. We lift each other up, not tear each other down.

I do want to add, just because I was not able to speak to the king in him at the time, it didn't make me less of a woman. I can say this based on two reasons. One, I was not ready or whole and two he was not a good fit for me. He didn't speak to the queen in me either.

I won't resort to breaking my own crown. There are enough broken crowns out here. It hurts me to see the brokenness in my queens because we allow brokenness to be our driving force and base many of our decisions on it.

Now my question to you is are you walking in queenship? Do you have the character traits of a queen? Take a minute and take an inventory of your character traits and see. I have provided some journal space just for you. Fill it out and let's talk after.

My Queen Behavior (My Thoughts)

_____

_____

_____

_____

_____

_____

_____

_____

_____

_____

_____

_____

_____

_____

Chapter Two

Wholly Dedicated to Being Whole

"A relationship will not be fulfilling when you are not experiencing it as a whole person" ~J.B. Allen

Are you whole? The word wholeness means the state of being unbroken or undamaged. So, I ask you again Queen, are you whole?

Women are natural nurturers. We love hard. Because of this, we leave our spirits open to a lot of vulnerabilities. We are very emotional beings. We also can bear much pain. Even more than men in most situations. It's as if we have a natural endurance for pain. Although men may feel the weight of the world on their shoulders, we have carried our own fair share of weight.

Some of us are carrying the weight from our last relationship. We have not managed to let go of the pain bequeathed upon us, from our last divorce. Many are being broken down to pieces in current relationships, even as we speak. Are you whole? Ponder on that question for a moment.

I have had to ask myself that time and time again. Especially, as I watched my second marriage going South. In my first marriage, my excuse was, "We both were young." It was just that, an excuse for another failed relationship. The truth was, we both were broken. I found myself bringing that brokenness in each relationship after it and leaving each failed relationship with a little more of me broken and damaged.

As my second marriage was starting to fail and was headed for divorce court, I had to take a pause. I knew I would be the common denominator of two failed marriages if this one ended up in divorce. So, it was time to take accountability for what I was bringing to the table. It was then that I realized how broken I really was.

As I began to evaluate myself, I saw how I was being triggered by things my husband was doing that reminded me of the man who walked out on me before him.

Those things angered me, and I would lash out at him. My husband, my King, was carrying the burden of another man's garbage, that had hurt me. It got even deeper than that.

As I begin to seek professional help, I realized I was carrying the weight of things that had happened to me when I was a child. Things I had not let go of. I found out I had daddy issues along with other things.

Those issues became the driving force behind how I dealt with men. They were the foundation of the wall that I had built inside my heart towards men. They drove my decisions concerning my relationships. With these as a foundation, how could I even fathom the idea of getting into a relationship? I was damaged goods.

Am I alone? I don't believe so.

Now many may have come from healthy homes with fathers who reminded them of the princess they were. Homes where they were affirmed regularly. What I have seen is that even in those situations those beautiful queens were not prepared nor taught that some men would not treat them like daddy did. That these men would contradict everything daddy said and break them. Because of this, some of my queen sisters' entire worldviews towards relationships and men, have been skewed. Queens, it's time to be made whole again.

Becoming the best version of ourselves starts with healing. To heal we must be honest and get to the root of matters of our hearts.

Let's begin by being wholly dedicated to becoming whole. This is for us and no one else. Wholeness includes mind, body, and soul. Let's begin to deal with those things that have had us bound and damaged. Let's begin to let some things go and walk in forgiveness. Let's give ourselves time to heal before embarking on something new.

If you are already in a relationship let's start the healing process right where we are so we can look at everything clearer. Let's give ourselves a real chance at Eros love by walking in wholeness. I have to say this queen, "damaged goods are not an asset in a relationship."

To become a better version of yourself requires knowing who you are. Having your own identity outside of a relationship is imperative. It's about getting to know yourself. To begin this process, you must take an honest approach. You must see yourself for who and where you are at the time. Boy, this part can be hard and can hurt. But Queen it is needed. That mirror is our friend and biggest enemy sometimes, but it tells the truth. Use it. Look deep to truly see you. Get to know her.

This has less to do with the outer man, and more to do with the inner man. Get past what is on the outside because that truly is not where your true self lies. You, the you, you should get to know, starts from the inside out. Learn that part of you. If you look deep enough, you'd be amazed at what you'd discover.

The more you learn about yourself the more you'll discover those things that have kept you from being great. You'll know what needs to be addressed and dealt with. It's time for our minds to be renewed and our hearts to be restored.

If we don't allow this process to take place before rushing into something new, we will hold someone else accountable for another person's garbage. That is not fair to you or your king or future king.

As broken vessels, we lose our identity. We don't know who we are anymore. We become needy for validation from men. We become like chameleons.

I remember watching a movie, I think it was called "The Runaway Bride", I am not sure. Nevertheless, in the movie this young lady would become engaged to different guys, before running away from the alter. I don't remember much about it, except whenever she was with a guy and they ordered their eggs to be cooked a certain way, she would claim that was her favorite way of eating an egg.

The young lady didn't know who she was. She had lost her own identity in the relationships. Honestly, she certainly should not have bounced from one engagement to the next. It was obvious she needed to be healed from something.

After being rejected by a man we began to question ourselves. We began to question if we are good enough or not. Asking questions like, "What's wrong with me?" I have the answer to that question, Nothing! There is nothing wrong with you queen. Hurt people hurt people. Brokenness plus brokenness equals brokenness.

This is why wholeness is so important. This is why understanding and embracing your queenship is important. Thinking like a man is a non-factor.

Are you whole queen? If not, are you really ready to impart into or impact someone's life?

When it comes to wholeness it's okay to be selfish. This is one of those times, so you're good.

Let us heal so we will recognize our kings. Both parties should come to the relationship whole and ready to add to someone, not take away from them.

Ladies, there are a whole lot of Boaz' (good men) out there looking for their Ruth, their queen. However, so many of us are carrying baggage full of mud from the last relationship.

One of the worst things we can do is invite someone into our lives knowing we are not mentally or emotionally ready. It's not fair to either of you.

How do we heal emotionally? First, we forgive. Starting with forgiving ourselves. How do you forgive? First, by taking yourself out of victim mode. You will never heal if you remain a victim.

Personally, I had to understand that my father had his own issues and everyone who hurt me, including me, did also. I had to forgive people for being people. People are people.

Many times, if they don't have anything that restrains them, like religion, self-control, or other methods, anything goes. When I began to understand that I began to let things go. I also learned some things about myself in the process. I am wholly dedicated to becoming whole. I am finding freedom in the process. It's time to be whole.

Queens, have you noticed the first few chapters are about us? Accountability begins here, with us. Why are we wasting time trying to think like a man to get into their heads, and trying to make them choose us; when we don't even know who we really are ourselves?

When you are sure about who you are, your worth, and all that good queenliness you bring to the table, there is no need to think like him. You think like a queen and speak to the king in him. If he is your king! Ooh, that is deep.

Make sure he is even your king, that is first. The one you're with may not be "your" king and that's ok. Your king will know how to speak to the queen in you. There is a king out there who desires a queen, just like you, trust me. Just be ready to receive him, as you are wholly dedicated and determined to become whole.

Chapter 3

Thinking Like a Man

"If we were supposed to think like a male God would have made us one." J.B. Allen

Ladies let me tell you a true story. Once upon a time, I wore size eight jeans I had a nice body. My waistline was snatched, and I thought I was all of that and a bag of Frito lays with dip. I wore tight clothes and high heels every day. My weave hung long down my back and my make-up was put on nicely. As some would say, "My face was beat to the Gods." Back in those days, I was crowned "Neighborhood Hot Mom", for three consecutive years. Back then I believed I could have any man I wanted. To be quite honest I just about did, and I am not bragging. That is an entire book by itself. SMH (Shaking my head).

Back in those days, I conditioned my mind to think and act just like a man. I had been advised to do this by some of the men I dated. So, I did just that. I thought just like them. I thought the way I imagined a man thought, and let me tell you, I was a straight mess, in need of a holy ghost deliverance session.

When I ask most women about their perception of men, many have the same response,

"Men are dogs!" I can honestly say, "I was no better."
I was a cute poodle dog with the bows and red
fingernail polish, cute, yet still a dog!

Back in those days, I bored easily with one
man. I didn't believe in giving my heart to one man.
Even when I tried, there would always be so much
drama in the relationship, that it wouldn't survive.

My way of thinking had been conditioned by all
the experiences I had with men, including my father.
As much as I loved my father and miss him, (he is
deceased), he abandoned me in many ways. He
wasn't around to teach me how I should behave like
his little girl. Men taught me how to behave. Let me
be frank, they were not great teachers. I was
conformed to think just like them. The way I
assumed they thought, at least.

Let me tell you, it hurt me, more than it hurt
them. Eventually, I found out my beliefs about how a
man thinks were all wrong and misconstrued.

The bottom line is I didn't trust men at all. I
believed I would do unto them what I predicted they

were going to do unto me. But again, I was totally misguided. You see, all men are not like that. As a matter of fact, there are many good men out here, we just need to understand them.

During my little think and act like a man phase, what I found out was, men are very fickle, as I mentioned earlier. They are very emotional beings who have issues with expressing themselves. Men suffer in silence. Many are truly overwhelmed and are looking for the same things we are looking for, support! Many have been scarred by cute poodle dogs with bows and red fingernail polish.

It has been stated, "Men are driven by who they are, what they do, and how much they make." I'm not so sure that is all that drives men. I believe men are also driven by insecurities, doubt, and an invisible weight on their shoulders. Many are driven by trust issues as well. This perpetuates their inability to express how they are truly feeling inside, so they bottle all of it up.

Then many men expect their women to help them fix (them) or give them the peace they are seeking. If she is not capable to oblige, they look for it somewhere else.

That is my take on it, but I asked my husband if I was on track. He agreed with me on many points but corrected me when saying, "help to fix them." He removed the word fix and replaced it with build their confidence. He believes men are driven by the pressures of life that are naturally placed on men. He believes the greatest asset to a man is a queen that knows how to make him feel comfortable enough to express himself freely, without being subjected to ridicule. He says when a man can look back and his queen is standing behind him, having his back, that is a gift.

I said to him, "Aw that's so beautiful baby." But as he walked away, I went back to my first thought.

Many men want their women to help fix them or at least make life feel easier for them! This has nothing to do with having an inability to think like them because we really can't anyway. There is not one woman who knows what it feels like to be a person who was born a man.

There are men out here who have that cheerleader, as my husband calls me, behind them, and they still are not happy. They are continuously being driven by that void or unfulfilled place in them that they don't have a cure for. So, queens don't beat yourself up when they cheat or spend twenty-five years determining if you are the one for them. *Sidenote: That last part is truly the most hurtful. My heart goes out to that queen who waits an entire lifetime for the man she loves to make her his wife or significant other. It is hurtful. Queen, I want to say to you, "It has nothing to do with you. That is all on him." But I digress.*

Many of our kings don't recognize the king in themselves. Then many are just selfish, as many of us are. Some are bigger divas than some women are, as defined as important to self only.

Said all of this to say, "All men are not driven by the same thing." They have different experiences, therefore, will have different worldviews. They see life through different sets of lenses. It is impossible to think like them.

Therefore, I believe it's imperative to know yourself first and have a mental idea of your expectations of your man. If not, you will find yourself questioning your queenliness.

Many queens are trying to figure out, right now, why that man doesn't want them. They are questioning if they are pretty enough, sexy enough, or have done enough, or should do more to please him.

Some of my queens are trying to figure out why he cheats. They are wondering if they are woman enough to keep him interested. The saddest are those who are questioning if it's them that makes him angry enough to strike them. *Abuse is an automatic disqualifier, but I digress again.*

Trying to think like him will have some of us all over the place. Some of you queens are doing way too much. The man ain't even asking you to do most of the stuff that you believe he wants. You're at his beck and call. Some of yall sucking toes too, let's be honest. Giving him bathes, which can be fun. You're keeping it sexy and tight for him.

Some are even compromising who you are for him, and he still seems to be unhappy, cranky, a miserable person, and in other women's inboxes.

To be honest, some of you are trying to wear too many hats to please your man, when all he wants is someone to possibly bounce ideas off of, a shoulder to cry on and not be considered weak, or just wants someone to support his dreams. He wants someone he can just confide in. He just wants to know he has a strong woman that can hold it down if he gets down. Some men need their queen to keep them balanced and grounded. Tell him when he is wrong and when he is right. He needs someone to celebrate him when he is worthy. He needs someone who can create a safe space for him. A place of peace. The man has been fighting the world all day he should not have to fight with you too.

Ladies, we can get so caught up wrapping our entire world around his world, that when he needs us, we are incapable of standing up, because we don't know our own strength or who we are. So, he is forced to keep going, even when he feels like he can't go any further.

We will discuss this in an upcoming chapter, "Succeeding at Something."

Queens if you want to know what your man is thinking, ask him. Try some impromptu conversation starters. "How are you feeling baby?" "How was work baby?" "Honey is there anything on your mind you'd like to talk about?" Even an occasional, "You good?", won't hurt. There are so many others. Be creative queens.

We don't need to think like men. We do however need to understand them better. You don't have to think like a man to speak to the king in him.

That is a skill only a queen can master.

Chapter 4

Acting Like a Lady

"Transforming the outer-man without reforming the inner-man
is like pouring new wine into old skin. It won't work! J. B. Allen

I was born in the sixties but grew up in the seventies. I grew up admiring Diana Ross, Lena Horne, Diane Carrol, and Gladys Knight, who was my absolute favorite, and other greats, like Donna Summers. These queens would dress so elegantly, in their beautiful gowns, when they were performing or were invited as guests on shows. They were the epitome of queenliness and elegance, externally.

Not sure how their internals was set up, but on the outside, they were queens. As time passed and female liberation emerged on the scene, we have become more unapologetic about how we carry ourselves. Social media has not helped this.

Queens first impressions matter. Let me repeat, first impressions matter. We have all heard first impressions are lasting impressions.

This chapter will not be long because I am not here to use my momma voice on anyone. I am here to share my experiences. Because of my experiences, I believe I am qualified to speak on the importance of acting like a lady.

Transparent Moment: *"Before God delivered me; I loved the company of a man. I dated many many men. Men of different races, cultures, religions, and backgrounds. As I said before I thought just like them and treated them just like I believed they treated women. My heart was never in the equation. I erred on the side of acting like a lady and it led me to many bad mistakes and decisions. "*

So there. Now you have read my credentials to talk on this matter.

Back to where we left off. First impressions are lasting. When Diana Ross and others came on the stage, they were jaw-droppingly beautiful. Y'all know some people love themselves some celebrities, right? Nowadays these celebrity idols walk on stage and it's also jaw-dropping not because of beauty but booty. It's becoming hard to watch.

Ladies, it doesn't matter your stature in life, if folks' first impression of you is that you are a...What's that word Santa Claus uses when he is on the sleigh, "ho, ho, ho" ...yeah that's it. If they think that you are a Santa Claus phrase, that impression can be lasting. There is a thin line between being sexy and being seen as promiscuous.

Somewhere in a jungle, in the rain forest, in a cave in a mountain, there is a queen who is walking around with no clothes on. Her twin girl parts, under her chin, are swaying freely from side to side. All she has on is a leaf covering her secret garden. While her moon pie is feeling the breeze along with her girl twins. Guess what, where she is from that's cool. It's in style. That is how they get down over there. Where I am from, they have names for queens who dress half naked (refer back to Santa). I'm just saying.

Queens being a woman doesn't qualify us as being a lady! There is a level of accountability that comes with being a lady. There is a difference between those two words. Being a woman qualifies your sex (female), only. Being a lady qualifies your character and the way you carry yourself.

As important as your external attributes are, your internal traits are just as important. As far as the external, ladies when it comes to our dress, more is more. Let's leave some things to the imagination. We can dress modestly and be gorgeous at the same time. We don't have to push our girl twins up to our nose hairs, to feel glamorous. But maybe some queens believe they do? That is why I am here. I want to remind you that you are a beautiful queen.

Many of us focus on being sexy and we believe sexy means showing some skin. Well, that may be true because some synonyms for the word sexy are erotic, sensual, racy, suggestive, and stimulating. I for one will never look at the word sexy the same again.

Ladies, there is a time and place for sexy and it's certainly not when you are trying to convince someone you are a lady. Sexy sounds like it belongs in an undefiled bed with a husband, and not at Walmart. Ladies more is more. Don't allow the desire to be seen as sexy to disqualify the right for you to be treated like a lady.

When I had breast, (I am a breast cancer survivor, double mastectomy), I wore clothes that showed a lot of cleavage. It never garnered the respect I desired from men. Many men looked and gawked at me, but few respected me as a lady. But that is my story. It may not apply to you. But for me, it just didn't work in my favor.

Some men like for their queens to be more modest in dress, while others may like to use their queens as trophies, as Queen Vashti's man tried to do. You see what happened to her when she said, "No." He kicked her to the curb. But she never compromised, did she? She was like, "Boy Bye!"

I change my mind; this chapter may be a little longer than first anticipated. I think we can stay here for a little while longer.

Now don't get me wrong I do believe in being sexy for your husband. But I must be honest I am not always sexy. Sometimes I look like someone's thrown away auntie. I just don't have the energy for all of that, all the time, anymore.

However, it is nice to keep it tight for your man behind closed doors. What I am talking about right now is when you step outside those doors. How you carry yourself matters. When you are out in those streets you are not representing a man or your man; queen you are representing yourself! Act like a lady queen. "Your Queenliness Matters."

A lady dresses to impress not attract, there is a difference. I am not sure what kind of attention you are looking for, but the way you dress, and act will determine what kind you get. Just my experience.

When someone addresses a woman as a lady, they are addressing that woman with a level of respect. A lady is defined as a woman who possesses class, self-respect, and other positive attributes. This woman watches her mouth. She doesn't speak all kinds of vulgarities.

Oh, my goodness when I tell you before God did a new thing in my life, my mouth was filthy. I didn't care whom I spoke vulgarities to, minus my elders, I always respected them. Outside of that, I had no self-control. When I look back over my life, I regret how I spoke to my children.

My mouth certainly disqualified me from wearing the title lady. I had to fix my tongue.

A lady is open and honest, speaking her mind with tact. Speaking what's on your mind is not vulgar. Being able to communicate openly and honestly is a big deal. Being timid doesn't qualify you as a lady, like being strong doesn't disqualify you as one. Queen your presence alone should demand respect.

A lady keeps herself clean, which includes having good hygiene. Now I must admit that some days I do not brush my teeth for the recommended two minutes, but that's my business. Moving on.

Hygiene is important. We all have different body chemistries. You'll have to find products that match yours that keep you smelling fresh.

To the queens who are married, single, and ready to mingle, or in a relationship, the way your house looks matters. In other words, "A Clean House Matters." Now I must admit I am not the cleanest queen around, but I cannot and will not live in straight filth. Untidiness and filth are two different things.

I remember when I worked in property management and one of my tenants called the office complaining that the young lady next door to him was disturbing him, by banging on the walls and playing loud music. Come to find out he had played with her emotions and decided she wasn't what he wanted. She was upset and was trying to get his attention.

Well, as part of my job I had to go and investigate what was going on. As I walked the corridor, I could hear loud music blasting from her apartment. So, I knew he wasn't lying about the music. Once I approached her apartment, I knocked on her door. When she opened the door, she was shocked to see me. I was also shocked at what I saw. The way this young lady, with children, was living was ridiculous.

There was dirty laundry from the front door to the bedroom, on the floor. Garbage was piled up in the kitchen. Dirty dishes were piled up. The house was filthy and had a stench. In my mind, I was like, "Sis you don't have time to court nobody you need to be cleaning up this house." How could she even bring someone in there? I left perplexed. I just couldn't understand how a young woman could live like that. Honestly, how anyone could?

Queens, we cannot honestly walk in queenliness if we are living in filth. I must admit sometimes my clothes get out of hand. Just recently, for the second time, the clothes rack on one side of my walk-in closet fell to the floor. Clothes were all over the place. Honestly, I have no room for all my clothes. I have too many clothes and shoes. But that's my business too! My husband and I are trying to figure out a new design for our (my) closet, to support my clothes and shoes.

Nevertheless, what I have found is when I am overwhelmed with things, I tend to get messy. I try to avoid dealing with things and it convolutes my mind. When my room is messy or untidy, I'm usually hammered in thoughts. Sometimes I must breathe and regurgitate some of those thoughts. In these moments I must remind myself that the things I cannot change I have to pray about and leave them at the foot of Jesus.

Sometimes our minds just need a reset.

Another thing is, I have a big house. Sometimes trying to clean it all by myself is overwhelming. I spoke up and just told my husband that I can't do it by myself anymore and I was hiring a cleaning company to help and guess who will be paying for it?

Queen to Queen, I am not Hazel, Florence, or Jeffrey. I didn't sign up for that. I signed up to be a helpmeet. Not "The Help." Therefore, I need help. Girl, It can be overwhelming.

I'm sure I am not alone in that. There are many queens out there that have full-time jobs, raising kids and running a house, while creating a home. Many are alone and some are married. Life can become a lot. So, sometimes we deal with issues by not dealing with them, for a spell.

Then other queens avoid issues by cleaning. They clean and clean and clean. If you walk in some of your homes, we are blinded by science (the fumes from bleach, Fabuloso, and ammonia). I'm just saying!

The bottom line is cleanliness is next to Godliness, according to John Wesley. Although this quote is not biblical, it most certainly is true. Queens, we must find a healthy way to declutter our minds, our lives, and our homes.

Ladies, please stop getting upset if your man doesn't want to hang around a filthy house. It really can be a turn-off. Especially married women. Stop getting upset at your man. If it is too much tell him to help or hire someone to help you. It's ok to communicate that to him.

Now let me sidestep for a minute. If you are sharing a space with someone else, then cleanliness is half their responsibility. Unless you are a stay-at-home mom, wife, or other, and cleaning is all you must do. If not, both parties should share that responsibility.

Now I am not trying to hurt anyone's feelings. I am trying to help somebody. It's probably better to not invite anyone over until your house is clean. First impressions, remember.

But you know some kings will come in and help you out. They may figure, that is not your strength. They may like to clean. They may but everyone doesn't think like that. So, it's best to try to tidy up for yourself. Let's be clear keeping your house, car, and body clean is for you, not them. To be honest, a lot of clutter around depresses me. I just don't like it. Do you ever feel like that?

A woman that gossip is, well let's just say, gossiping is not attractive. There are many verses in the bible about gossiping. The one that stands out to me is Ephesians 4:29- "Let no corrupt communication proceed out of your mouth, but that which is good to the use of edifying, that it may minister grace unto the hearers" (NKJ).

Ladies, I must be honest I hardly trust a person that gossips, especially about another Queen. We are here to fix each other's crowns not to damage them. So, let me clear up what a gossiper does. These people have unconstrained conversations about other folks, spreading information that may or may not be all true. That is not an attribute of a lady to me.

I pride myself on having a drama-free life. One of the reasons my life is drama-free is because I don't participate in gossip. But once upon a time, I was a "she said, he said", kind of person. I was much younger, but I was. My life was filled with drama. I didn't like it. So, I reduced my circle and monitored my conversations. It has been peaceful.

The last attribute of a lady, according to me, is she loves to fix another queen's crown. She is not in the business of damaging her sister. Therefore, being a side-chick, well let's just say, it damages another queen's crown. If you are the weekend chick, you are not his lady or his queen. Again, I am not here to hurt or damage another queen's crown. I am here, to tell the truth, and to help somebody.

There is no such thing as a glorified side chick. Don't allow social media side-chick groups, men, or anyone else to convince you of that. It is not so. Even if you get that man, and damage another queen, that first impression of you will always refer you back to Santa. You are too valuable for that.

Acting like a lady and walking in queenliness go hand in hand. Being respected as a lady is a big deal. That title not only warrants respect, but it demands it. Carrying yourself as a lady has nothing to do with a man, that is for you, queen. Remember that!

Chapter 5

Succeeding at Something

"When you walk in the truth (God's truth) of who you are, you walk

in the best of who you are! Be whom God created you to be" J.B.

Allen

Hey, beautiful I have a couple of questions for you. What are you doing with your life? Do you have dreams or aspirations? Are you pursuing them or watching others live out their dreams and succeed at things? Would you consider yourself successful? If you answered, "yes" to the last question, then you are on a roll. If you answered, "no", we have some work to do. Good news, there is time.

As a youngster, I would hear people saying, "learn to mind your business." It was important to know how to mind your business. Now if you don't know what that means, minding your business simply means to concern yourself with what concerns you and not others.

To be honest, I had not always mastered how to mind my own business. I was always distracted by what other people were doing and their business. Other people's business always seemed more interesting to me than my own. Because I was doing absolutely nothing with myself for a while.

I stayed in drama, gossip, and relationships that added no value to my life. I was going nowhere fast and wasting a lot of time on the way there.

I had to get some business of my own. Starting with doing things that would add value to my life. In my younger years, I didn't feel successful at anything I put my hands on. I worked mundane jobs that left me feeling unfulfilled. I even acquired my cosmetology license to pursue a career in hairstyling but didn't feel confident in that. I was really scared to tap into my talents and step out and do something that took courage. But one day I became "woke" and did just that.

By thirty, I was a single mother raising three girls. I didn't have an education past my high school diploma, with a 1.95 GPA. I was not college material back in those days, so I enlisted in the military at nineteen years old. Which was a Godsend for me because I was a drug addict with nowhere to go at the time. The military opened some doors for me, but it wasn't enough. I was going nowhere. I wanted more for my life and wanted to plant seeds of inspiration and hope in my daughters, by being a role model for them.

At thirty-seven years old I enrolled in college to pursue an undergraduate certificate in business and contract negotiations, and never looked back. I did complete the certificate, went on and got my bachelor and finished my **MBA** with a 4.0 **GPA**. But I ain't done yet! I am minding my own business and have plenty to mind.

When I met my husband, at forty-two, I was already established. I had my own good credit. I was paying my own bills. I had my car. I had my own good government job. I wasn't looking for handouts. Compared to some, I was seemingly successful from the outside. But I wasn't done. I was just getting started.

In the early parts of my marriage, I was on a sabbatical from what God had called me to do. To be quite honest I think I dumbed myself down, so my mate wouldn't feel insignificant. He never asked that of me. I did it voluntarily and it almost broke me internally. I needed to get back to minding my business. Because I was finding I had too much time on my hands minding his. I was nagging him all the time and was on his back constantly about one thing or another. But that's my business, (laughing emoji goes here).

I'm saying all of this to make a point. Instead of waiting on a knight in shining armor to rescue you, be about your business. Succeed at things that make you proud of yourself. Have your own accomplishments. Tap into your own gifts. You be great when he meets you. Or better yet, walk in your greatness even after you've met. Don't stop being great because you are in a relationship. Let me tell you something, there is more to being a virtuous woman than wearing purple.

Amid writing this book, I began to dive into Proverbs 31 to learn more about the lady we call a virtuous woman. This woman, who was described, in the Bible did not go by the name, she went by deed. She is known to us by character and deeds only. That is intriguing to me. That a no named woman, or a mere description of a woman of the past, could impact our lives, as women, so much.

Proverbs 31, mentions King Lemuel, whom many speculate was King Solomon. King Lemuel was never mentioned again in the Bible outside of this poem. Therefore, for this book, I am going to assume King Lemuel is King Solomon and he is sharing, in a poem, things his mother spoke with him about.

In this poem, he describes to the reader the type of woman his momma wanted for him.

Not to get too deep into Solomon's past, but Solomon was a player. He loved women, exotic women. The Bible described many of these women as foreign. So, from what I can tell, Solomon was about that swirl life. Although he was considered a wise king, his weakness was women.

His mom tried to advise him, when he was young, about the kind of woman a king should desire.

You all know how we mothers are. We don't believe there is any woman good enough for our sons. We warn them about them fast girls hanging around them and to be careful when choosing their queen. Well, that is what Solomon's mom was warning him of in Proverbs 31, amongst other things.

She made it clear to him that looks, and body are not the qualities of a queen. She explained that it is the character and attributes of that woman that makes her queen worthy. She wanted him to seek out someone who could add value to his life. Someone he could be proud of.

A queen or Proverbs 31 woman has certain qualities, you are not able to find in any and every woman. Solomon's mom Bathsheba broke them down for him.

I have heard many sermons about the virtuous woman or Proverbs 31 woman, but when I studied her for myself, I realize this chic is a real boss. Even in biblical times, she was described as boss.

Outside of having spiritual and practical wisdom, she was God-fearing and had high moral standards.

Now before we dive into my perception of a virtuous woman, let me first say this. Although many align a virtuous woman with a wife; I believe this woman is a boss before marriage. With that being said let's begin.

The poem doesn't begin to describe this woman until verse eleven.

Verse 11) The first thing it says is she was trustworthy and faithful. She knows how to carry herself around other men and in public even when he is not looking. He also doesn't have to hide his money from her because she is wise when it comes to finances. She is not cleaning out the bank account buying Dooney bags and Louis Vuitton shoes trying to keep up with the Jones, okay? He trusts her to pay the bills on time.

Verse 12) This woman knows how to have her man's back. She is a real ride-or-die. She knows how to speak to the king in her man.

Verse 13) This is where she bosses up. She works to add income to the household. She has her own career. She taps into her gifts. She is not lazy. Lord now that part stepped on my toes. Because I can be lazy sometimes, but I call it resting (but that's my business).

Verse 14) She feeds her family more than McDonald's and Kentucky Fried Chicken. Seems to me she wants them to eat healthily. She knows how to cook! Sis, you don't have to be a gourmet chef to prepare a meal for your family. If you can boil water, you can cook. I'm putting together a cookbook to help some of you queens out. Even my vegan Queens. Look out for it.

Verse 15) She is an early bird. She gets up early to handle her household business. What strikes me is this verse implies she has employees and knows how to treat them too.

Verse 16) This chic owns real estate. She is financially literate. She is smart.

Verses 17-19) Remind us of how hard she works. She has her own business. She is described as a seamstress. But you can be an author, speaker, teacher, life coach, and make beautiful flower arrangements. Whatever it is, the world is waiting.

Verse 20) Describes her unselfish behavior. She helps those less fortunate. Now to do this you have to be in a position to bless others.

Verse 21-22) Reminds us of how much she loves her family and herself. She makes sure they are good.

Verse 23) shows us how she gives her husband bragging rights when he is with his boys, based on how she carries herself and treats him. Not only that, but her influence has added value to his influence in their community. Come on now. A real boss chic.

Verses 25-28) Remind us how strong she is. This woman can stand in the paint for her family when things get tough. She is wise. She is not caught up in childish gossip because she is minding her own business. She speaks wise words and kind words. This Queen is respected at home and in the community. Her character demands it.

How many are virtuous Queens, really? This is doable. You don't have to be married to be her. Honestly, my belief is for you to already have your own business *(not in the literal sense)* and succeeding at something before bringing your king into the picture.

Also, you don't necessarily have to have a business to be this woman. This has nothing to do with external success but internal success. Succeeding on the inside starts with having a sense of self-fulfillment and pride. Are you genuinely proud of who you are? Or is there more work to be done? If you are not all the way there yet Queen that is cool, because God ain't done with none of us yet. Keep it moving. Keep being great!

CHAPTER 6

Your Mental Check List-Setting Your Standards

"When you have established (set) standards and expectations you are not walking into a situation with an empty canvas" J. B. Allen

Sometimes I go to the grocery store without a grocery list. Whenever I do that, it causes me to spend more money than I set out to spend every dead blasted time I step foot in a store. I am constantly throwing things in my basket I didn't go to the store for. Don't let me go in there hungry or thirsty. My Lord that is even worse. Has that ever happened to you?

You go into the store hungry with no list and find yourself wanting any and everything you see. Get home and empty your bags, pull out Pimento cheese like, why in the world did I buy this I don't even like Pimento cheese like that. Shaking my head.

Most of the things we pick up are not even good for us, but we just want it so bad in that moment because it looks so tantalizing. Sometimes I'd pick up a snickers bar to get a quick fix. Or other things I have no business eating.

That analogy kind of sums up how we go about this dating game sometimes. We have no mental checklist of what we want in or from a man. We just are out here winging it. Many times, ending up with pure junk.

I remember a line from the movie "Waiting to Exhale", when one of the young ladies was breaking up with her friend and he shouted out to her, "You need to be careful whom you be picking up from the grocery store." That is about the only line I remember from that movie because it stuck out to me so much. Hey, he was telling the truth.

I can honestly say when I eat before I go to the market, I buy less, and can stick to my list. That is a strategy for me. I prepare myself to go to the market to avoid overspending or ending up with things I didn't even want.

I have a similar strategy with dating. I found a way to mitigate the possibility of picking up or ending up with an "L" (loser). What I did, is first made sure my mental state was in check. What do I mean? I made sure I was not going out in those streets hungry or thirsty. Secondly, I had to have an idea of what kind of man I believed would fit my personality and life.

You see if we don't have an idea or a standard/bar set, we will find ourselves going into a relationship trying to conform grown men into what we think we want. Then later finding it was all for nothing and an extreme waste of our time. We don't have the power or authority to change anyone. I will be discussing this in the next chapter, "Fixer Upper Syndrome."

You see both men and women must have an idea of what they want in a mate or significant other. With a mental checklist already established, you'll have something to line your suitor up against. Now let me say this; our mental checklists should be reasonable/attainable with some wiggle room for compromise. Now there are ways to compromise without lowering your standards.

Ladies I have to say this also, "most" men have a good idea of what they want in a significant other. They have an idea of the kind of lady they will bring home to meet their momma and marry. They also know the kind they will lay and play with. Men may be some divas sometimes, but they know exactly what they want and don't want most times. We must catch up!

Queens, we are natural nurturers, well most of us are. I am not sure if that is a blessing or curse for us. We tend to love our kings with our entire hearts. Because of this many of us are more than willing to give potential a try. We fall in love with potential. Some are probably thinking, "So what's wrong with that?" Well, it's nothing wrong with it, if that is what you'd like to do.

Let me define to you what potential is. The noun definition has potential as hidden qualities or abilities that "may" be developed. The keywords there are "hidden and may."

Therefore, potential is just like faith, without putting them into action they are dead. Potential means nothing if it stays hidden. The person must want to develop what is hidden in them. Many times, by a certain age, if they haven't, they most likely don't want to or have no interest in it.

A man can have the potential to be a one-woman man. However, if he likes to date multiple women at one time or is a cheater, his potential means nothing.

I once dated a man that was sixteen years older than I was. He was in his late fifties when we kicked it. This guy was still hanging out in clubs every weekend; and was always concerned about his fashions. He was living in a one-bedroom apartment and had no car. I believe his cell phone account was in another man's name, which was suspect. He had children and children's mothers but never wanted to be married. He instead liked to swing with different women of all ages; having to continuously dye his hair and mustache black, to avoid revealing his true age. But hey kudos to him for being able to pull it off for so many years. When I last saw him, he was in his sixties, doing the same thing, I assumed. By this time, I was married and had no further dealings with him.

He had the audacity to be upset with me because I had gotten married. This guy was full of potential, but he refused to bring what was hidden inside of himself to live.

I am not knocking giving people a try, but from my past experiences falling in love with just potential has left me broken and regretful. A man must bring more than potential to the table, like his own self-respect, self-love, spirituality, mental well-being, an income (legal tender), a car, and a dream at the very least. Just saying!

Now I am not being hateful when saying this. What I am saying is, if he has no dreams, visions, or good intentions for you, you two are unequally yoked, and he brings nothing to enhance your life, outside of sex; queen he is not the one.

If loving him means losing a part of you, then you may need to re-think the situation. Loving someone should never cost us anything. It should add to our lives. Allow him to get himself together then come to you. Just as we should be whole when we explore a relationship, so should he.

Now to be honest I don't know what is worst, falling in love with just potential or a straight fixer-upper.

I must say it, some of us just go for the underdog. We honestly believe if we get in the mud with him, we can help bring him up with a shower and a shave and he will change. We overlook the fact that maybe he likes being in the mud. Everybody doesn't want to and isn't willing to change for us. They like where they are. Some are comfortable where they are. They don't know anything different. I will discuss the underdog in the next chapter "The Fixer Upper Syndrome."

Queens, I'm sure you already know if a man abused the last woman in his life, chances are he will abuse you. If he was a cheater when you met him, more than likely he will cheat on you. For any of us to change it takes a mindset change and a renewed spirit. Without it, real change is not possible. It's not easy to give up comfort zones!

When I think of our mental checklists, they would be equivalent to a job listing. When a company or manager lists a job opening, they generally have a good idea of what a good candidate looks like. They have an idea of the qualifications, attitude, and persona they are looking for in the right candidate for them. We should see our mental checklists the same. They give us an idea of what a good fit looks like to us, for us.

It doesn't guarantee we will end up with the best fit, but at least it gives us something to work from. We can easily disqualify the ones who haven't made the cut.

When we go out in the streets with nothing to guide us, we are liable to pick up anything from the grocery store.

CHAPTER 7

Fixer Upper Syndrome

"Some projects cost more than they are worth" J.B. Allen

This chapter will be a short one. I just wanted to be clear on what I meant by fixer-upper syndrome in the event you need to examine your current situation to determine if your man fits the description.

What is fixer-upper syndrome? I am glad you asked. Fixer-upper syndrome is when a king or queen tries to build a relationship with someone, they know is unsuitable for them, but they pursue it anyway. Be advised I made that term up. But it certainly sounds scholastic.

What is a fixer-upper? I am glad you asked that too. A fixer-upper is a person that comes to the table completely damaged and broken with absolutely nothing to offer. For example, like when you are introduced to his family and the family looks at you as if something is wrong with you because you are dating him.

The saddest thing about fixer-upper syndrome is it is usually not about the other person, it's about us. This syndrome aligns so closely with Munchausen

Syndrome, (when a parent makes a child sick just for attention). Fixer Upper Syndrome is an attention seeker as well. We put our hands deep in the miry clay and pull out the most damaged person we can find so we can feel special.

Many queens do this to feel valued. They believe if he is broken enough, ugly enough, or low enough they don't have to worry about him hurting them. In the queen's mind, she feels he should feel lucky to have her.

Well queen I 'm here to say anyone that is not adding value to your life, but is taking something from it, is hurting you.

I want to tell you a story about a girl. This girl dug way down in the miry clay and got her man. He was at the bottom, but he was cute to her. He could never keep a job but could find one every other month. His biggest downfall was he smoked crack. She dressed him up in nice clothes just to find out he was selling all the new clothes she bought him for drugs and resorted back to wearing his old raggedy sweatpants he wore daily.

He was bringing her down with him. Although she had fixer-upper syndrome bad, she was getting tired of him. It all hit the fan the day he stole the key to the church she attended, the key pastor had entrusted in her care and stole all the church's computers leaving her with pure humiliation and shame. But she gave him a chance even after that great humiliation and ended up with an even greater humiliation when she ended up in jail for trying to run him over with her car. She had to call the same pastor for bail money and prayer. She eventually left him to get someone even worse.

This was a mindset issue. This girl is not alone. So many queens do this. They seek out brokenness to feel make themselves feel whole.

What I find sad about fixer-upper syndrome is a queen who goes into relationships like these usually has issues with deep-rooted feelings of unworthiness. There is a void in them that usually deals with some abandonment issues. They believe a person at the bottom would never leave them because they assume the person on the bottom could never do better than them.

What is even sadder is the queen doesn't want them totally at the bottom. How do I know this? Because the queen does whatever she can to build him up, so he is more presentable in the public eye.

That may mean getting him those new teeth, and clothes, and giving him a little pocket change, or whatever is needed; so, they don't look like who they really are.

These queens are afraid or intimidated to deal with men that would be on their level, above, or more suitable because they believe they would not feel as valued or bring value to that type of relationship.

This is why it is imperative to succeed at something in your life. It's imperative to be whole and succeed on the inside of yourself. It's important to know your worth. You need to have pride. When you know who you are and are successful in your own right, you are not intimidated by a successful man. One of the characteristics of a queen is she walks in confidence. How is your confidence level queen? If your queenly meter is off a bit, then it's time to fix your crown. Walk in confidence.

I am not sure if you have seen the Property Brothers on HGTV. Well, they spend a lot of time fixing up old, damaged properties.

They start with a budget but in many cases end up spending way more than they budgeted for. It's because many times in fixer uppers there are so many hidden issues deep in the foundation of the homes. It seems once they discover one issue and fix it here comes another.

After watching that show I realized if I ever bought a home, it would never be a fixer-upper it up can be time-consuming and too expensive. The Property Brothers make it look glamorous on tv, but in real life, many people start projects in their homes to never finish them. They leave them half done because the projects become too exhausting.

Queens, I must warn you fixer-upper syndrome does not protect you from heartbreak and disappointment. Your fixer-upper can get fixed up and start to believe he is too good for you. These projects (men) can also turn out to cost more than they are worth.

CHAPTER 8

If it Feels Like Abuse, Looks Like Abuse,

Then It's Abuse

"We should never waste life on things that add no value!"

J. B. Allen

Since the beginning of time, starting with Genesis 3:16, where God told Eve that Adam would rule over her; we women have had to prove our significance and worth. We have sought out validation from our male counterparts.

We have had to fight for the right to vote, to have careers, for equal pay, equal rights, our right to choose, our right to have a voice, and human rights. Some of our fights are even deeper depending on the race and ethnicity of the queen.

Many of our sisters are still in deadly battles, fighting for the right to just dream. Our Afghanistan queens are in my prayers constantly. They are in the battle of their lives right now and I stand with them.

Ladies let's be honest society has attempted to make us feel like secondhand citizens compared to men. It's sad to say, but this is even in the House of God (Christian Church). When I grew up women were silenced in the church.

All the men sat high on the pulpit while the women could not step foot on it, except to serve the men. Times have changed since then, but not a whole lot.

Women have been degraded in song lyrics. Described in a less than appealing fashion and made to feel like they are replaceable. We have been body shamed. Made to feel we must look a certain way to be deemed beautiful or sexy, which motivates us to get cosmetic surgery and make other cosmetic modifications; that ends up still not good enough.

African American queens are mocked for wearing weaves and lashes as they are trying to live up to these expectations of what men deem sexy. My Caucasian queens are mocked for getting lip enhancement surgeries for the same reasons.

All of this has somehow pitted queen against queen in constant competition to be the baddest chic. Why? In most cases, it is to get our male counterparts' attention. Let's be really really real we have been bamboozled by society!

This has had an impact on our psyche. Subconsciously we don't realize how all of this has impacted us and still does. If you ask me, it is self-imposed emotional and mental abuse.

Do I think that all these things put together have conditioned our worldviews into thinking we are not complete unless we have a man's attention or last name? Yes, I do. In many ways it has. That is why reconditioning our mindset is important.

Before my words are taken out of context, let me assure you that I am not saying this to bash men or marriage. I am only trying to convey to you how worldviews are formed and how outside influences are almost always the main components of how we view ourselves, relationships, and men.

Much of this book has been comical but this chapter is such an emotional one for me. As you can see in this chapter I want to expound more on abuse. That would include emotional, mental, and physical abuse.

What is abuse? I am sure we all have an idea of what physical abuse looks like. It's not hard to define.

Physical abuse is when your partner hurts you by causing physical pain...e.g., (slaps and punches).

Many queens accept physical abuse as a gesture of love. I knew women who believed if a man didn't beat or show some adverse emotion towards them, the man didn't care about them.

They considered their man's hot temper, as a sign of jealousy, believing a little jealousy is cute. Abuse is not about being jealous, it's about being in control.

Examples of emotional and mental abuse are, yelling at you, being a habitual cheater, calling you out your name, and gaslighting (manipulating you into questioning yourself, narcissists are good at this). Abuse should be an instant disqualifier. But unfortunately, in many cases, it isn't. Why? Great question. I believe we have a way of normalizing abuse. How? Another great question. I believe it's because we either grew up witnessing it in our household or have found a way to dumb it down and accept it as being normal. There is nothing normal about abuse.

Being loved can be a beautiful experience and we all desire it because God created us that way. When I think about love as God has defined it, it seems perfect. Sharing life with someone who shares the same sentiments about love, makes true love appear attainable. But what is love? To me, true love is an action. A word that requires acts of love. Respecting me is an act. Treating me like a lady, holding me in high regard, is an act. Disrespecting me is an act as well and is a counter to respect. What is a form of disrespect to me, you ask? Any form of abuse is disrespect, including infidelity. There is power in an act. It impacts our emotions whether the act is positive or negative.

In an earlier chapter, I spoke about how nurturing we can be as women. Men think they must protect and provide. As women, we think we must take care of everyone. That characteristic can be tricky when dating or considering a lifelong partner.

Compassion can easily lead to compromise, and as I said before too much compromise can dissipate the bar of standards we've set. We can easily find ourselves investing in ways to help "him" change. This turns into a vicious cycle of self-inflicted pain and disappointment.

It took a long time for me to learn that the only person I could change from the inside out was myself.

I can recall staying in relationships I should have run from because I thought patience was the answer. "Just wait, change is gonna come", I'd tell myself, but it never came to pass.

Sometimes when I look back over my life and recall some of my experiences, I believe I should have taken heed to the advice Ms. Sophia gave Celie in the movie Color Purple, "You betta bust Mista upside his head and think of heaven later."

Now let me be clear I am not suggesting anybody bust Mista upside his head. So don't say J.B.

made me do it. No violence is needed. We just need to decide and stick with it.

We must know when to go. We must recognize when it's not a good fit. We must understand that some people do not want to change and it's not our responsibility to convince them that change is good. Some people like who they are. Even as swine in the mud; they like it.

Jesus told us in Matthew 7:6, not to give what is sacred to dogs and not to throw our pearls to swine. He went on to say that if we do give them what is sacred like our hearts, our bodies, our time; they may trample them under their feet and tear us to pieces.

Our savior is truly the only wise God. We must be ever so careful when casting our pearls to the wrong person because it surely could leave us damaged and broken into pieces.

Scorned queens, those who have felt the aftermath of casting their pearls to swine, complain about all men being dogs. That is far from true. It's just many of us have given up what was sacred to dogs. There are some good men out here, very good men. All men don't have the same mindsets.

Besides ladies, we can't get upset with swine for being swine and acting accordingly. That is all they know. It's their nature. We just spoke about fixer-uppers in the previous chapter and will discuss red flags in "Don't Cast Your Pearl a Bad Investment."

I remember dating a guy that would physically abuse me. Each time he'd beat me or hit me he'd ask, "Oh I guess you're going to leave me now?" Each time I would stay, thinking, "he just needs someone to have patience with him and understand his pain." Ha! When his pain began to cause me pain, is when it was time for me to go. But I stayed until one day I got the courage and had, had enough. Not only did he beat me, but he also cheated, and tore me down with words. There are so many levels of abuse.

As women, we can honestly spend a lot of time trying to get our men to see our worth. We try to convince them that we are keepers. We cook and clean for them. Give them our entire hearts, and they still aren't happy. Many will still cheat, misuse, and disrespect us. Why? That's a good question. I believe it's because we allow it. That is the only answer I have.

Some of us have believed that having their babies would keep them home or turn their hearts to love us more. Not so! If they aren't willing or better yet, ABLE, it changes nothing. There must be a renewing of the heart and most times the mindset in them.

Many of us ignore red flags with hopes that with patience will come change. In many cases, the change does not come. Why change when I can get what I want being whom I like to be? That would be my question. If there is no incentive to change, why would they? I will discuss red flags in the next chapter, "Don't Cast Your Pearls."

I am reminded of the story in the Bible about Leah and Rachel, Jacob's wives. They were sisters.

Yes, two sisters were married to the same man. Now you know that was messy. If you'd like to read more about Jacob and his wives, you can find the story in Genesis 29 beginning in verse 15. As I said it gets pretty messy.

To make a long story short, Jacob was tricked into marrying Leah the oldest sister, but he loved Rachel, according to the story. That is whom he wanted to marry. Jacob eventually married Rachel also.

The story goes on to tell us that Rachel was barren, and Leah was giving Jacob his sons. Each time Leah birthed a child she prayed that Jacob's heart would grow affection towards her, but it never did. She gave him son after son and still, he only loved Rachel. What I found striking, is the story never said Rachel loved Jacob. The one who loved him, he didn't love. The one he loved possibly didn't love him the way he loved her, but I digress.

One other point the story tells us is although he wasn't in love with Leah, he honored her at the end of her life burying her amongst his ancestor next to him. At a point in Leah's life, she began to take her eyes off Jacob and focused on God. He buried Rachel, the one he loved, on the side of the road. Lord men are fickle, aren't they?

My point of this is babies do not guarantee love. Birthing children with men who don't love you can be a nightmare for you and the child. Think twice about that.

Facelifts and cosmetic surgery only satisfy a superficial desire. Which are usually short-lived. Women have had butt lifts; tummy tucks and their men are still not satisfied with them. They still cheat, many times with someone whom some would consider less attractive. Which proves superficial things will never keep him grounded. Unless he is superficial himself. There is never substance in those relationships.

Men want something deeper. Real men, that is. Even over-sexualizing your relationship will not keep a man satisfied. Been there done that and it didn't work. Sex alone gets old too.

Queen just like Leah, at some point you must take your eyes and energy off a man who is not willing to love you the way you desire to be loved. Go into the situation understanding you will either accept him as he is or not at all. If he is not what you want don't invest. If you do, you may find yourself settling, left broken, compromising, or all the above. There is no situation worth that kind of sacrifice.

CHAPTER 9

Don't Cast Your Pearls a Bad Investment

"You take big risks investing in junk bonds. The same

risk   applies in junk relationships" J.B. Allen

I was on social media the other day and came across a post that had me shook for a minute. So, the post said something like, "If I want you, I don't care about your past or your issues. Don't tell me that I am not able to handle your issues let me decide that." I was like hold up did I just see what I think I saw?

So, the man is telling you that he has issues. Issues he believes are not fair to bring to your table and you are upset with him for not giving you a chance to help solve his issues or allowing you to decide if you want to live with them or not? I must be honest queens that post didn't make any sense to me. I am a believer that if a person tells you something about themselves, believe them.

I remember when an ex warned me, not told me, but warned me that he was not ready for what I wanted, and it was best he hurt me a little bit then, by walking out of my life, then a whole lot later. I didn't take heed to his warning and invested anyway and was devastated after he hurt me a whole lot more later.

Investing your time, heart, emotions, and money in someone should take an equal amount of consideration as would any investment. Maybe even more. Love is a gamble just like the stock market.

However, with the stock market, a smart investor would only gamble with the house money. They would not invest everything they have, banking on a win. That is where the stock market and relationships differ. With relationships, we usually go in, all in.

I agree once you are sure about your king you should go in with your whole heart. That would be fair to both of you.

However, before making lucrative investments in anyone, you should be paying attention to any red flags.

The time to do this is while getting to know a person. This is when you are determining if the two of you are a good fit for one another. Going in with full investments before making these observations is like putting the cart before the horse.

In business, world leaders are tasked with the responsibility of hiring people to perform certain duties within their organizations to meet organizational goals.

During the selection, process leaders are interviewing many candidates. All the candidates present themselves as the best person for the job. Leaders understand that most candidates are not going to reveal everything about themselves during the interview. They know that hiring people for jobs within their organization comes with some risks.

If you are trying to get a job, you probably won't disclose to the interviewer that you were fired because you stole from your prior boss and will steal from them too if given the chance. It would be the honest thing to do, if true, but not the smartest. You will probably not get the job.

Leaders rely on resumes, background checks, and references to get an idea of who they are about to hire. They do this to avoid making an adverse selection. They also pay attention to signals, like if the interviewee has a degree or other experience they are looking for in a candidate. Leaders do this to avoid investing too much time and money into the wrong candidate.

In the dating world, we too have signals called red flags. Red flags are all we have, outside of background checks and word of mouth, to warn us of a possible adverse selection. Red flags are our friends, ladies. Red flags caution us and keep us from making bad decisions that could cost us later. At least that is what red flags should do. What I find stunning is we tend to treat our friends, red flags, as enemies and many times ignore them.

Queens, we all enter relationships with asymmetrical information (one person holding all the information about themselves). Some people are not willing to disclose certain things about themselves even deep into the relationship. That is why it's imperative to pay attention to red flags. Just like managers, we can't just rely on what people say or we could easily make an adverse selection.

If we are not careful, adverse selections can cost us dearly. That is why it is important to know your worth, know how you want to be treated, have an idea of what's a good fit for you, understand that changing someone is not an option, and avoid overlooking or ignoring red flags.

All red flags aren't deal breakers. Some of us can deal with one thing, while others can deal with other things. We all have our tolerance levels.

Now queen we know most suitors are not going to come out the gate spilling all the tea about themselves. He is not going to say, "I have bad credit." "I am no good." "I ain't never treated a woman right my entire life." "I beat women." "I'm a liar." "I'm still married and I ain't leaving my wife." "I'm dead broke." "I just lost my job and need somewhere to stay." "I've told six different women, God said I was their husband knowing I was lying."

Ladies, they are not spilling that kind of tea. But if they do; sis run for your life. (Laugh emoji goes here).

All jokes aside, we must find out as much as we can about them before we haphazardly cast our pearls and make too big of an investment. Let's Pay attention to things like:

- How does he handle his mother?
- How does he carry himself?
- Is he trustworthy?
- Are his habits tolerable?
- Does he have coping issues?
- How does he treat you?
- How does he treat others outside of you?
- How does he communicate with you?
- How does he handle his kids, if applicable? Does he have good relationships with his children?
- Are his values and yours compatible?
- How does he handle his bills?
- Is he self-sufficient or always asking to borrow money from you and others?
- Does he have dreams and ambitions?

- If you are a Christian, is he and, are you two equally yoked?

These are great questions to consider.

Transparent Moment:

There were a few red flags I noticed when I was dating my husband. Not huge flags but flags that should have been addressed. There were flags on both sides. I'm sure he saw them with me too because I was damaged goods and fighting a very hard battle with cancer when we met. We ignored our red flag and got married. Because of this, we have had an uphill battle getting (us) healthy. Things are good now. But it's been hard work!

Ignoring red flags can add to the work that is already required in relationships. It just makes it harder.

Some conversations need to be had before moving forward. If not, we can find ourselves going into the relationship trying to change someone to make them fit and find ourselves losing who we are in the relationship and being left with broken pieces. I keep bringing this up because I have seen it time and time again. We always seem to leave a piece of ourselves behind.

Jesus warned in Matthew 7:6 "Do not give what is holy to the dogs, nor cast your pearls before swine, lest they trample them under their feet, and turn and tear you in pieces."

Although in this text He was speaking to the disciples about the gospel warning them not to give what is holy to people who will not find any value in it. He was saying, "don't waste your time." The same sentiment and scripture can be applied here.

Don't cast what is sacred to men who will find no real value in it. Your body is sacred. Your heart is too. You are sacred and valuable. The warning was that everyone won't understand your value. Pigs will drag your pearls in the mud. But can you blame a pig for it if that is all they know to do?

We spoke about "fixer Upper Syndrome" in an earlier chapter here I want to talk about "Sugar Daddy Syndrome." I made that up too. I describe it as when a woman chooses a man based solely on his assets. When you believe finding a man with money or one who knows how to get that bag will solve your problems. Both syndromes can leave you empty.

When you focus only on outer appearances or tangible things and not the mindset of the person you are setting yourself up badly.

I have heard so many sad stories of women depending on men financially who are left feeling lonely and miserable. But because they purposely ignored red flags to get in where they fit it, they are living with the repercussions now.

You can't ignore red flags. If you see the pig, then you hand over your pearls to the pig, you can't get upset when they are trampled on. We must take responsibility for our decisions. Many of us know before we go, but we go full speed ahead anyway. Many times, we do this because we fear being alone. I will be discussing the difference between being alone and loneliness in the next chapter "Alone Does Not Mean Lonely."

The fear of being alone should not cost us everything. It should not entice us to hand over our pearls to men that are not deserving of them.

I know what I'm about to say will sound a little harsh, but I have to say it. Ladies, it is time out for having compassion for dogs and pigs. Let me repeat pigs and dogs get no compassion. I'm not talking about our beautiful pet babies. I'm talking about men who choose to act like untamed, undomesticated pigs and dogs.

In the real-world pigs and dogs have very little control over their animal instinct or nature, unless they are trained and even then, it's just in their nature to adapt to the ways of their species. These animals have very few choices.

However, the men who drag our pearls in the mud have a choice. They are choosing to do just that. Do they deserve compassion? I don't think so. Compassion is defined as having pity or sympathy for the misfortune of others and having an understanding. Based on the definition compassion is not fitting. Forgiveness yes, after you've moved on but not sympathy.

We all know when we are behaving out of sorts. We know when we are acting mean, disrespectful, etc.

We sometimes believe being understanding towards them is a way to get them to recognize their ways and do better. Some may try, but many won't. Some people like who they are.

Jesus warned the disciples that if they invest their pearls (time, heart, body) into those who will never find value in them, they would be left hurt and trampled on. I believe the same applies to us. He is wise.

The one thing a woman has is intuition. We know when it doesn't feel right, it probably isn't. A woman's intuition is a gift God gave us. It is up to us to use it as it was meant to be used.

We should treat relationships and dating like stockbrokers treat stocks. Stockbrokers are not in the business to lose. They are in the business to get a return on investments. We should be in the dating business/relationship with the same idea. Let's not invest in anyone who cannot guarantee a return. He should add value to your life outside of sex and superficial things. If sex and superficial things are all he brings then queen, he may be a junk bond.

CHAPTER 10

Alone Does not Mean Lonely

"Being alone, outside of a relationship is not a curse. It truly is in how you look at it" J.B. Allen

I spent most of my life witnessing society make barren or single women feel devalued. I've heard single women, in their late twenties and older, being referred to as spinsters and old maids. While single men, of the same age, are simultaneously deemed eligible bachelors and or players. That has always been bogus to me. It certainly is not true.

Society has made it seem there is something wrong with being single and something noble about being married or attached to someone. Yes, being married can be nice if you have the right person. But so can being single. It is good and bad in everything.

Some act as if being single is a disease. I don't understand that mindset because, to be honest, I liked being single. I thought there was so much peace and calm in my life when I was single. I only had to concern myself with my children and myself.

I found the only time I felt overwhelmed with being single was when something went wrong in my house, or I was having issues with my car. Other times were when I was financially broke, and felt I was facing the world all by myself. At times I felt I just wanted to be a woman, not an independent strong black woman, just a woman, and have a man take care of me because I was tired of doing it all by myself. Then something happened. I learned to be ok with doing it all by myself and I did it all by myself.

I became! I learned to enjoy my company. I had no problem with going to dinner or a movie alone. I enjoyed my me time, even now. Although I don't have as much me time as I did when I was single; I still enjoy the time I can take out for myself.

Queens what I found is we tend to get the word alone mixed up with lonely. I don't care if Oxford's and Webster's dictionaries claim these words are similar. They are not. Alone means physically being by yourself. While lonely means you are sad you are by yourself. Two different meanings.

If you feel like you are more of the latter my question to you is, "Why?" What makes you sad when you are physically by yourself?

I posed this question to my daughter, who is still single, and asked her to share her experience with me. This is what she wrote to me:

"My single woman journey has been very challenging. I can understand the fear of being alone or not having anyone. However, one thing I've learned while being single was "myself." Through my journey, I noticed how I lost myself looking for a relationship. I found myself settling for relationships I should have stayed out of. I found myself vulnerable and susceptible to insecure men that tried to tell me who I was and my value in this world. I see now how women are broken even in relationships and find themselves falling victim to misery.

However, going back to the fear of being alone. I found myself feeling lonely when I dated men that were empty. I realized it was better for me to continue to work on myself, alone. I am certain that sooner than later my person will match me. To be quite honest I have found power in being single. When you have choices, you have power.

What's funny is men ask me out all the time. I've been invited to go on boat rides, jet skis, dinners, trips, and more, with no strings attached. You see the moment you get over the fear of not having somebody is the moment you realize you can have anybody. By the way, don't convince yourself that you've wasted time in a relationship that you had to cut off. You are gaining time. Each day you wake up you are adding time to becoming the woman you want to be."

Now my twenty-three-year-old daughter wrote that, and I didn't know someone asked her to go on trips and things. As I am typing her words I'm saying, "Huh?" But I digress. She was being honest and transparent. She knows first-hand how it feels to not have a significant other in her life. But she tells me all the time that she will not settle. She says she will wait on her match to come.

I believe the more you become, the more they be coming.

One of my favorite movies is "The Last Holiday" with Queen Latifah and LL Cool J. In the movie, Queen Latifah who plays Georgia was given a false diagnosis of cancer. When she thought she only had a few weeks to live she decided she would live out the rest of her life on her terms. At the time of the diagnosis, she was working in a department book and only had a book of possibilities. Before this excursion, she lived a mundane life waiting for her crush, played by LL Cool J to confess his love to her.

She decided to take all her money out of savings and retirement and splurge. Without notice, she took herself on an exclusive vacation away from her everyday life. During this time away she discovered things about herself she never knew. She wasn't concerned about anything but herself but found herself building lifelong relationships with strangers. The love of her life came looking for her. By the end of the movie, she had found out that the diagnosis was a false positive. In those weeks of risk-taking and just living life, her life became one worth living. Once she focused on herself, everything she ever desired came to her. Her renewed mindset changed her entire life. I love that movie.

Just like Georgia in the movie, I notice when I focused less on finding a man, and more on discovering who I was, the man found me.

Now I don't want to sound like one of those married women who try to lecture single women on how to wait. That is why I had my daughter contribute to this chapter. I remember when I was single and the married women would lecture me, so I am familiar with how demeaning that can feel.

The truth of the matter is God designed us to desire to be loved and to reciprocate that emotion. We were built like that. However, as my daughter expressed giving love to the wrong man can make you feel lonely times ten.

Your match is out there. However, some of you may need to change your mindset. What do I mean? I mean instead of looking for a man decide to wait on him and in your waiting love on yourself.

Love yourself in such a way that your man's love for you will compete with your love for yourself.

When I met my husband, I was not looking for a man. As a matter of fact, before meeting my husband I was diagnosed with breast cancer and had just had my left breast removed and had started chemotherapy. I was in the fight of my life. The guy who abandoned me, after I was diagnosed, told me I wouldn't be any good for any man after I lost my breast. I must admit, as much as I didn't want to, I believed him. I didn't think a man would be interested in a bald, sick woman with one breast. So, I postured myself to be alone and was fine with that at the time.

I was still wrapping my head around being 42 years old with one breast fighting cancer. That was a hard pill to swallow.

Well, I'm here to testify I was wrong and so was the guy who abandoned me. Come to find out some men are not that superficial and know how to love the whole person.

I met my husband at work as I was walking back to my desk, and he was walking to see a friend. As we passed each other in the corridor, our eyes met. We had worked in the same building for almost four years and had never seen each other before that day. The following day he made his way to my desk. He found me. We were married four months later. The rest is history. I must add that the first date we had was at one of my chemotherapy sessions. He took off work to accompany me there because I hated going alone.

I know I'm amazing, but I still wonder why he took that kind of interest in me at that time in my life. But I digress.

My point is at the time we met I wasn't looking. I was happy in my life. God had lifted the burden of fear off me about dying and I began to live. I joined Zumba. Began to eat very healthily. Went to the gym. I spent quality time with my children. I was just enjoying the presence of God in my life and bam, there he was. Out of nowhere my baby came and got me.

As I said before, as you began to focus on yourself and whom you are becoming, they will be coming. Just wait with anticipation and joy in believing your match is on the way to get his queen.

CHAPTER 11

Who Says?

"We limit love when we try to keep it in a box" J. B. Allen

I am going to keep this chapter short because I already know this chapter will be a little controversial, but I am going to say it anyway. As I am listening to Robin Thicke's song called, Sweetest Love, I want to talk about dating outside our race.

For a long time, I was very apprehensive about the thought of marrying someone outside my race. As a matter of fact, I use to hate seeing accomplished black men dating outside their race. I was one of those sisters who would be mean mugging at a brother who had a woman outside of his race, on his arms. As I have gotten older, I realize how wrong I was. I learned we must not limit love by keeping it trapped inside a box.

As I mentioned in a previous chapter, I enjoyed dating. I didn't discriminate when it came to dating. I dated men of all colors and races. I was beautiful, single, and ready to mingle, back in the day. I'm delivered and married now but haven't always been, but I digress.

Nevertheless, I learned something from all the different cultures. People can be interesting. It amazes me just how different we are yet so much alike. All of us bleed the same. All of us experience life the same. We experience the good, bad, and ugly. We all have the same senses and experience joy, pain, hurt, and disappointments that come with living.

I am so ashamed of my prior mindset. I was so out of bounds. But I was taught to think like that. I was taught that I was only allowed to date, black men.

When I was about sixteen years old my wonderful grandfather, whom I love dearly, made me promise him I wouldn't marry a white man. My grandfather thought he was sparing me from hurt, harm, and danger. So, because of that promise, I would only date white men, but I would never allow myself to get serious enough with them to marry. I hurt good people because of this mindset and who knows how those relationships would have turned out had I not had that mindset.

Now don't get me wrong I do not regret marrying my wonderful, good-looking black man. No regrets at all. He is my Boo. I am also not attempting to make amends for the decisions I made concerning interracial relationships. What I am trying to do, however, is to hopefully get you to think outside the box.

I would hate for any queen to miss out on love because of traditions, myths, or someone else's prejudices. It wouldn't be fair. Love comes in all kinds of packages and different shades of color. Real love should not be restricted by color.

I remember when I was in the military my platoon was deployed to South Korea in the winter months. Man, it was cold over there. At that time, I was dating a black guy but had dated a white guy before this relationship. It just so happened that all of us were stationed in the same area at the same time. As I said it was very cold at the time. Although the white guy and I were no longer together, I remember him finding me. He found me to bring blankets to keep me warm. He looked really hurt when the black guy I was dating pushed me inside the tent and wouldn't allow me to take the blankets. I never saw him again. I never got blankets from the guy I was dating either.

The black guy and I broke up. He was emotionally and mentally abusive, but that is another story.

I am not telling this story to bash black men, because I absolutely love my brothers. I'm sharing this story because although the guy I was with never showed me that kind of beautiful love I stayed with him and overlooked a tender and beautiful love from someone else, because of his skin color. The white guy was always sweet to me, but I just couldn't see past his skin color. Wow, it truly hurts me even today when I see his face standing there with those blankets. Wow....

Queen if a man is interested in you and asks you out to dinner or a movie, lunch, brunch, or a picnic in the park please don't allow his skin color, or creed, to be the determining factor. Treat him like you would treat any man. Treat him like a man, not a white man, black man, Asian man...just a man.

CHAPTER 12

Don't Drag His Pearls

I am writing this chapter while listening to Boys to Men's "On Bended Knee." Yes, sis, it's on repeat. I love that song. As I listen, I'm pondering this thought; Queens sometimes I think we forget or possibly have never realized that men have feelings and emotions just like a woman. They hurt. Their hearts get broken, just like ours.

Women are deemed to be the weaker vessel, physically. Honestly, I believe when it comes to the pressures of life, women just handle that better. This could explain why the suicide rate amongst men is three to four times higher than that of women in this country. Unfortunately, men usually suffer in silence.

Men are experts at holding their emotions inside and can sometimes react like children when they are overwhelmed. Whereas women are the opposite because we tend to wear our emotions on our sleeves.

I think much of the pressure on men stems from the fact that men have been convinced that they are responsible for carrying all the weight on their shoulders. Society has taught men that having a woman in their lives, or a family means they are responsible for all that concerns of that woman or their family, especially when it deals with finances.

I'm sure that alone can be very intimidating and can be overwhelming, for some men. 1 Timothy 5:8 says, "Anyone who does not provide for their relatives, and especially for their own household, has denied the faith and is worse than an unbeliever."

Now, this is the New International Version's version of the scripture. In King James, the verse identifies the (their) as he and his. If you apply one of the principles of hermeneutics here and interpret this scripture literally, it will make it seem that the entire responsibility of the family is on the man. That is not what the scripture is talking about. It's talking about the care of widows, elders, and the poor within the family. So, we are all responsible for that believe it or not.

Outside of this scripture, I was not able to find one scripture that said the man had to pay all the bills, make more money than their significant other, and take care of everything. Trust me I searched. If 1 Timothy 5:8, meant what many may feel it means it would be contrary to Proverbs 31.

I do believe for a man to be deemed a good man he must be a good leader. Biblically a man is supposed to lead his family with the wisdom of God. But I also believe as his woman we are to make that task less daunting.

As we discussed in an earlier chapter the woman described in proverbs 31 was a go-getter and was very successful. Her husband was described as a man that brag about his wife. She handled her business. So, in that situation, that man had a helpmate.

I guess you are wondering, exactly what this has to do with the name of the chapter," Don't Drag His Pearls?" Well, I will tell you.

I started this chapter this way to give you an idea of some of the baggage a real (good) man comes into a relationship with. When a man loves a woman, he wants to please her. He wants to be the man he believes he is supposed to be to her, many times sacrificing to do so.

Men can spend so much time focusing on how to take care of their women financially and emotionally that they spend less time sustaining their mental health and spiritual needs.

Queens believe it or not, but please believe, there are many men out here, good men, looking for a good woman to settle down with and become one. Unfortunately, many times these men are overlooked and undervalued for whatever reason.

Another thing, many of us were raised to believe all men are dogs. That is far from the truth. As my husband said to me, maybe all the men we dated were dogs, but not all men are dogs.

Many of us also have abandonment issues because our fathers were not integral parts of our lives, so we have a lack of trust for most men. Then many of us have been devastated by someone because they were not our match, and we left that relationship broken and trying to put our pieces together. This is some of the baggage we sometimes bring into relationships.

In these new days and this feminist society, where women are making big major moves, some men can be intimidated by the fact that their woman makes more money than they do. That is a big one and one that has hurt many potential perfect matches. What's worse is many times as women we don't honestly know how to maneuver around that financial reality when we are in that situation.

In my opinion, the thing that makes that difficult is trying to figure out how to submit to a man that can't meet all your financial needs or living expenses. Well, it's simple, just submit. Submitting only means respecting him. Respect him enough to consult with him before making major purchases or major decisions. Respect his opinion. Never make him feel his opinion is insignificant because you don't need him financially.

I don't think we truly understand how that makes a man feel when he is constantly reminded that he is not needed. I tried to imagine if the man would feel the same way as a woman would feel in the same situation, but it really isn't the same. That feeling of not being needed can break a man to his core.

Queens, our men have pearls too. Why invite a man into our lives if we are only going to break him? If we want to preserve our man, we must protect his pearls. I for one do not want a broken man. Oh, my goodness, it's the worst.

We should be mindful of our actions and not make him feel like he owes us, or he has an obligation to us. Yes, we do have expectations but at the end of the day, that man has a choice.

Everything he does, big or small, is because he wants to. We should appreciate the small as much as the big. Anytime we can pour back into him, let's. Don't get me wrong I am not talking about settling. We will discuss how we should teach our men our love language in an upcoming chapter "Teach Him How to Love You."

Now I must admit when I decided to include this chapter in this book, I wanted to get into the mind of a man, so I had a little Q&A with my husband. He indulged me by sitting with me for a few and satisfying my curiosity.

Question: *Why do you think men hold in their emotions when with women?*

Him: *We hold in our emotions because some women can take what we say and throw it back at us. When you confide in a woman and she weaponizes what you have said to her and throws it back at you, it may make you /withdraw and keep your feeling to yourself.*

Question: *Do you think that does more harm than good?*

Him: *Yes, that's a possibility. If I was not able to talk to someone, I'd take my issues to God. You must have some kind of way to release.*

Question: Do you believe men think they have to carry the weight of the world on their shoulders?

Him: Yes, I think so. Especially black men. We grew up behind the eight ball. It seems everything we do we have to do better. Everything feels like a struggle. We are looked down upon. We must give 200% when it seems others only must give 1%. When you must deal with the outside pressures and then the internal pressures it can be volatile for some people and can cause emotional problems I would assume.

Question: Do you think you were raised to believe that when you are in a relationship with a woman everything is your responsibility?

Him: I wouldn't say with a woman, but with a wife. Society puts the weight of it all on the man, but when the man can't live up to society's expectations that is like a mental weight that is bogged down on a man. It can make someone feel like he is less of a man.

Question: *Do you think having a woman who makes more than you can make a man feel less of a man?*

Him: *Some men maybe, but not be. I guess it would only be bad only if I was constantly reminded of it.*

Question: *When a man feels like they are not needed does it make a man feel less interested in the relationship?*

Him: *I guess it could. Because the question becomes, "why am I here if you don't need me?*

Question: *Do you think unattainable expectations of a man can damage that man?*

Him: *Yes! Because if I can't live up to your expectations, because they are unrealistic for me, that can certainly mess up relationships. You know what you have when you get into a relationship.*

Although I had a good idea of how he would answer, I still appreciate my husband for lending me his ear and time for a moment. Sometimes it's good to get the information from someone who would know better than you. Bottom line our men aren't tin men. They do have a heart. In their hearts lies their pearls. Let's not drag them.

It took me a long time to get here. When I was younger, I handle men's pearls carelessly. I didn't understand the value of their pearls because I thought all men were swine. I devalued them. Even my husband at one point.

Transparent Moment: "When I met my husband, he made a lot more money than I did. He paid all the house bills. I paid for the in, like the car and health. That was all I had to pay besides my car payment, and I did buy groceries. Then God blessed me mightily in my finances with a promotion and other blessings. I begin to make more than my husband collectively. He still earned more than me, but I brought home more than him. My demeanor changed. I became meaner and careless with my words. I began to say, "I don't need you", to him, more often than not. Until one day he shut all the way down. He stopped paying bills. He didn't want to pay any. Oh, that got me heated. It caused a lot of friction in our marriage. I refused to take care of a man.

The word of God says in James 1:8, that a double-minded man is an unstable man, in everything. In this situation, I was being double-minded and it caused confusion in my house. Ladies a (good) man ain't going to want to be nowhere he feels he is not needed. We were both miserable. Then something changed. It was ME! I changed. I had to take my eyes off my husband and look at myself. The truth about healing is you are the first partaker in the process.

I knew either I was going to have to learn to deal with him not paying bills and being absent, which I could never do, or I had to figure out how to fix it, or I was going to have to walk away from the marriage all together. I prayed and God reminded me of why I fell in love with him in the first place. I knew my husband was a good man. He was raised that way by his father. But he had become someone I didn't know. I had to approach the situation differently if I was going to save my marriage. I will be speaking more about marriage in the upcoming chapter, "You Did, Now What?"

I began to talk to him about the man he had become and reminded him of the man he was raised to be. Then I took responsibility for any part I had played in his new conformity. I reminded him of how much I needed him in my life. I told him I needed him to be present. Because my husband is a good man by nature... he heard me. I kept reminding him of who he was. He and I eventually agreed on what each other's responsibility would be, as far as bills were concerned. I set attainable expectations for him. I knew when we moved to Florida my husband had an eleven thousand dollar decrease in pay. We had to adjust to that. It took a while, but we did. But since then, he has been promoted in position and pay. He is in a good place. Praise be to God.

I began to thank him for the little things he was doing, like washing the dishes. I would reward him by cooking his favorite foods. He loves to eat. I softened my heart towards him. Guess what ladies, on his own, he has been restored.

My husband now opens his heart up to me. He shares things about himself I never knew before. He trusts me. He barely allows me to pay for anything outside of what I pay monthly. If I ask for anything, he makes it happens. I very seldomly ask him for money. But occasionally I do because I think he likes handing me money. So, I stroke his ego and ask. It's a win-win for both of us. He is a good man"

Queens a man wants to feel appreciated and needed, just like we do. They have pearls, just like we do. Only wisdom can teach us how to handle our man's pearls. Let me tell you if you handle them pearls properly, there isn't anything he wouldn't do for you. A good man that is.

I don't have all the answers, but what I know is if you follow the principles of God concerning love, beginning with self-love, love will be reciprocated to you. Let your man know he is appreciated, and you have his back. You will experience him in ways you never have before.

Yall can come back and thank me later.

CHAPTER 13

Another Man's Garbage

We are all familiar with aphorisms that we've heard throughout our lives, like "one bad apple spoils the whole bunch." Aphorisms are observations that have some truth to them. Like the one, I mentioned above. Yes, it is a fact that one bad person's negativity can be a downer for everyone involved.

There is another aphorism I am sure many of you have heard. It says, "one man's garbage is another man's treasure." This aphorism originated with the idea that after someone has devalued an item and throw it away, someone else can come along and see something valuable. One person devalues it while another finds value in it.

We have brought that same concept into relationships and dating. I used to say that all the time when I would leave one relationship waiting for the next. "One man's garbage is another man's treasure." Many times, feeling like garbage after leaving the relationship, because either I wasn't ready or stayed too long.

Then one day a thought came to me. What if you were not the last person's garbage? What if you were a diamond even in that relationship but he didn't recognize it and didn't appreciate your value? My answer to those questions would be, "yes I was a treasure; it just wasn't a good fit."

I think when we speak this type of language when describing who we are, we devalue ourselves. This can go for king or queen. Our words are powerful and can manifest in our lives. That is why I try hard to be very careful with my words.

I am one to believe if we leave a relationship feeling like someone else's garbage, that can cause underline baggage. It sets us up to go into new relationships already feeling like garbage. I am one to believe if we just face the reality that it was just not a good fit for either party, it mitigates strife between the two people. However, I don't want to drag this chapter out by focusing on the phrase and the idea behind it, I want to focus on you queen.

The only way we leave a relationship feeling like someone's garbage is because we allowed them to treat us like it. That is why we must stand firm on what we believe we deserve. Even if you're married, you still have a right to have expectations of how you want to be treated. We will be discussing the importance of expressing our love language in the upcoming chapter, "Teach Him How to Love You."

Convincing your mind to think you were someone's garbage does more damage to you than them. That's why so many people have something negative to say about their ex. I don't understand that because all my exes and I have decent relationships. No, all my exs' don't live in Texas. But we do have decent relationships. The key to it all is "forgiveness." I had to forgive myself for staying too long in most cases. Then I had to forgive them. It freed me. It wasn't easy nor did it happen overnight, but it was certainly worth it. Forgiveness was the thing that unlocked the start of my healing process.

I must admit the person I dated before I met my husband had me feeling like real garbage. I left feeling like garbage and not thinking I was good enough for any man. As a matter of fact, he told me I wouldn't be good for any man. To give you an idea of why I felt this way; I am going to share an excerpt from my first book, my memoir "Hostage in the Mirror."

Before I share it, I want to bring you up to speed. At this time in the book, I had been diagnosed with stage 3 breast cancer and was trying to save my breast. The surgeon told me it couldn't be saved but I wasn't taking "no" for an answer. Do you want to know why? Although a mastectomy would save my life, I was refusing to get it done. It was because the guy I was dating at the time and shacking with, told me verbatim, "you ain't gonna be no good for no man with one breast."

How did I end up there? Well, I had recently allowed him to convince me it was a good idea for us to move in together after about three years of dating off and on. I lowered my standards for him by moving in with him. I had vowed I wouldn't do that with another man before marriage. However, I compromised this time under the consensus we would be getting married.

Well about two months before my diagnosis, he told me he wasn't ready to marry me. I was devastated! Then came cancer.

I was very reluctant to get my breast removed but knew it was the only way I could beat cancer. I knew I had to live for my babies.

Ok at this point in the part of the book I will share; I had just had breast surgery (removal of my left breast) and was in the hospital. I had breast surgery at about 7:30 AM that morning. *(I have changed the name to protect the identity of the person).*

Excerpt: *At 10'oclock p.m., Ron decided he would come by to see me. He hadn't been home all day. My children said he was out in my car all day and they hadn't seen him. I assumed he was out with* the new woman he was wooing. I knew when I was discharged, I would have to deal with it.

That is exactly what I did.

Before this cancer situation, I probably would have gone completely off. The undelivered Jennifer would have handled it with knives and police.

But that wasn't me anymore. When I came home from the hospital, I took it easy for the first day. I didn't say a word to him. I didn't even get upset at him as he watched my kids struggling to put me in the bathtub to bathe me. He stood in the kitchen eating a sandwich and watched.

My children took on the role of caregivers for me. I didn't have anyone else. I didn't want to be a burden on anyone, not even my children, but they insisted. My daughter Kailee was the headmaster caregiver. She measured and documented all the fluids from the tubes that hung from underneath my left arm.

The second day came. I asked Ron if he could stop and get the kids a pizza for me because there weren't any delivery services nearby. I explained to him the tubes made it hard for me to drive and cook. My chest and arm were very sore from the surgery I'd had a few days before. He refused because he said he was busy. I figured he was out with his boo. So, I asked God for strength, and I drove and got my children the pizza I'd asked Ron to get.

On the third day, his time was up. Without a second thought, I woke him up and warned him that he only had a few hours to get up, get his things and get out of my apartment. I must admit the old Jennifer was on stand-by because if he had bucked/resisted, I was going in full-throttle, tubes and all. In layman's terms, I was going upside his head regardless of the tubes or surgery. He knew I was serious and wasn't the one he wanted to play with. He had already met the old Jennifer once before.

I would not allow him to mistreat and disrespect me that way anymore, especially in front of my daughters. That was not happening. I didn't care *if I only had one breast. He needed to go and get him a woman with two breasts if that pleased him.*

Losing a breast was hard for me. It did bring on some insecurities because it was a new norm, I wasn't familiar with. With all of that, I refused to settle. God had brought me too far. I was hurt, but I knew I deserved better. It was for the best.

Queens that was one of the hardest times in my life and the hardest decisions I had to make. But I became woke. I was woken to the fact that I was not garbage. I was not less than, even with one breast. I was not unlovable. I deserved a love that could speak to the queen in me.

I must admit, because I had allowed this person who was not my match, to convince me that I was not a treasure, I went into my marriage with baggage. Jesus had to take the wheel because I was driving us into a ditch. But God.

I am saying all of this to say, even though the relationship didn't work out, you are still a treasure. You are no one's garbage. How could we be garbage when we are fearfully and wonderfully made? Ha! We were crafted in our unique design.

There is this Japanese pottery called Kintsugi pottery which is meant to be broken and mended together with gold. The meaning of Kintsugi is more beautiful and valuable only after being broken. That's you, Queen.

As a reminder, you are not garbage so refuse to allow anyone to treat you like garbage. You are shining like a diamond.

CHAPTER 14

Teach Them How to Love You

When it comes to love we must be bilingual~ J.B. Allen

"What is your love language?" The first time I heard that phrase I had no idea what they were talking about. Then my millennium children help me to understand it better.

A love language is a non-verbal way you give and receive love. There are known to be five different types of love languages, a concept created by a marriage counselor named Dr. Gary Chapman.

They are:

- Words of Affirmation
- Acts of Service
- Receiving Gifts
- Quality Time
- Physical Touch

There are many quizzes out there to help you determine what your love language (s) is/are. Based on Dr. Chapman, you can have more than one.

I personally don't think I need a quiz to help me determine how I want to be loved or treated. I am not knocking Dr. Chapman's philosophy about eros love, but I honestly believe the reciprocation of love should be based on how the other person wants to be treated. The only way you'll ever know exactly how someone wants to be treated, is by utilizing verbal communication. Or at least making it plain. No one, outside of God, can read our minds. Also, it's not fair to the person who is trying to love you, to try and figure out exactly what love looks like to you. We must teach them.

How do we teach someone else how to love us? It is not a simple task when the person you are trying to teach is not willing. However, if they are willing, it's only fair they are allowed to try.

The first is communication. This is key. If the person you are interested in is doing things that bothers you, tell him. Not by bashing mister upside the head, but with love. If it is a habit you don't like, discuss it. Not demanding them but explaining to them how it makes you feel.

Secondly, we must understand everyone wasn't raised alike. We have all been conformed by the environment we were raised in. At one time in my life, it was hard to say, "I love you" or give hugs. I wasn't raised that way.

It wasn't until I met my children's very affectionate grandmother, always giving hugs and kisses, that I was tailored to do the same.

For example, I have become a touchy person at times. I love intimacy. My husband on the other hand isn't as touchy. When we first met, he was a bit laid back and not the initiator. So, I had to show him. I initiated the kissing and holding hands. He now knows what I like. Now he will come over and kiss me in the mornings. He grabs my hand in public. You see I had to show him, and he had to be willing to adopt it.

At one point in my marriage, I would be upset about how my husband lacked affection. It was one of the reasons I was ready to divorce. I would fuss and fuss and didn't realize how I was chipping away at him. He shut down. But when I began to approach it differently. He began to respond positively. One day while taking pictures he grabbed me and had me sit on his lap. Ladies, he had never done that before. So, I know it's in him.

I understand that everybody wasn't raised the same. I wasn't raised with loving parents. As a matter of fact, I witnessed a lot of abuse in my family and had to deprogram my mindset from that before I could even identify with what true love looked like.

I know some would say, "Well I don't have time to baby my man." Well, I don't consider it babying him. I consider it as learning his love language and teaching him yours. I've been married for over eleven years, and I am still learning my husband.

When your significant other does something right. Let him know it. That will only motivate him to do it better next time.

I am always grateful for my husband's gestures of love. But recently I had to tell him that I didn't like flowers for a Valentine's Day gift. So, he gave me money and I bought what I liked. You see he was under the impression that every woman liked chocolates and flowers on Valentine's Day. Not me.

For years I didn't say anything and when I did, he obliged with no hesitation. He was like, "Ok I won't buy you chocolates and flowers this year", and I got what I wanted, and boy did I thank him.

When he does something right let him know and when he doesn't get it quite right, gently let him know.

Being willing to become bilingual in love languages is commendable. But before learning someone's love language, we must understand what love looks like. Love starts with *Philautia (Fi-lo-te-a) love,* or self-love. As I mentioned before I had to deprogram my mind and allow God to transform me and renew my mind before I could understand and properly communicate how I wanted to be loved. I'm reiterating this because it is important that we love who we are. The fearfully and wonderfully made person God created.

We need to understand and appreciate what makes us different. I'm one to believe once we embrace who we are we can communicate our love language with authority. We are not a clone of our significant other. Just because they like things one way doesn't mean we have to. Just because his love language is giving money doesn't mean you should not want him to still show physical affection towards you if that is your love language.

Now I want to add that if we are not healed our love language can seem unstable and wavering. We can throw folks off when we are back and forth and not even sure what makes us happy. Sis, don't drag his pearls, go heal. Because when our love language, or expectations in love, are unstable and unreasonable we can cause unnecessary damage to our partners.

Now, I think this chapter perfectly coincides with earlier chapters where we discussed how we should have our mental checklists readily available. Being loved the way you want to be loved is highly important for self-preservation. Being in a relationship that doesn't afford you that can be draining. This goes both ways.

I read a quote today that said, "You don't have to cheat to lose someone. You can lose someone from a lack of communication, attention, and disrespect. It's not always what you do, sometimes it's about what you didn't do" ~*Author Unknown.*

Our relationships do not have to lack if both parties are willing to learn each other's love language. If we treat each other not just like we want to be treated but how our partners want to be treated, then there shouldn't be an issue. Love was not created by God to be a burden but a blessing. All it takes is two willing participants.

As a reminder to love effectively these things are critical:

- Being a good listener- Listen to what they are saying. Also, hearing their hearts even when they are not speaking.

- Pay attention to their body language- Body language says a lot.
- Communicate.
- Learn their love language.
- Accept that everyone is different and have been conformed to their upbringing.

So, Queen if you are still trying to figure out what your love language there are plenty of quizzes out there to help you out. Once you have a better understanding of what your love language is; get to understand his. Then you two will be officially bilingual.

CHAPTER 15

You Did, Now What?....

Our wedding days are supposed to exemplify the life we are about to start with our husbands. We put every effort into the wedding day arrangements to ensure that our special day is as close to what a fairytale looks like to us, as possible.

Some of us like to make that day extravagant. We adorn ourselves in luxurious gowns gaining the attention of everyone in the room as we make our appearance.

Then some of us opt for a more intimate occasion. Small and quaint with a few close friends and family.

Then some of us elope into the sunset with our boo and keep it between the two of us until we are ready to share the news with the rest of the world.

Whichever way we decided to exchange our vows, most of us experience the same feelings of excitement, uncertainty, and maybe a little bit of good fear.

After the I/Do's are exchanged and the honeymoon is over the real marriage begins. This is when we find out that this new covenant, we have made requires a lot of work. Putting in the work does not mean it can't be just as beautiful as the day we jumped the broom. It just means marriage is not for the faint at heart.

Marriage is one of the most selfless relationships you'll ever have. You share almost everything. In marriages, there are great sacrifices and compromises. You will need to demonstrate all the characteristics of the fruit of the spirit according to the word of God. What is the fruit of the spirit? According to Galatians 5:22-23, the fruit of the spirit is love, joy, peace, forbearance, kindness, goodness, faithfulness, gentleness, and self-control. This is coming from the New International Version. Self-Control is crucial in a healthy marriage.

When marriage is practiced according to the word of God and love is performed according to God's way, it can be beautiful. Anything outside of that opens the door for all outside influences and a marriage filled with unhappiness. If you are in a beautiful, fulfilled marriage with your best friend that is wonderful. I believe that is what God intended marriage to look like.

Right now, I want to speak to that queen who is struggling in a complicated marriage. What do I mean by complicated? Well, a marriage that feels love-less. A marriage that lacks intimacy. A marriage that doesn't allow you to be who you are. A marriage that makes you feel trapped. Those are some examples of complicated marriages.

What do you do when you feel stuck? I think that questions can only be answered by the individual who is in the situation. However, I want to give you a little food for thought.

First, God did not intend for us to be mistreated in our marriages. Love begets love. Where there is no love, God does not exist because God is love.

Marriage comes with a great level of accountability, and it is not that easy to walk away. If you went into the marriage with divorce as an option, that was your first mistake. Divorce should never be an option.

Transparent Moment: "I have been married twice. In my first marriage, I went in with divorce as an option. I would always say to myself. "Well, I can always get a divorce", as if marriage is a game.

I tried to come into my second marriage with that same destructive mindset and almost ended this marriage on several occasions. I would always ask my husband for a divorce and guess what ladies he postured himself to honor it.

I would throw my wedding ring across the room all the time. Man, I was childish, but I digress.

One day I threw it across the room, and it went behind a heavy chest of drawers and God said, "Now go get it!" Even God was tired of me. I had to move that heavy thing and get the ring. God told me if I ever took my ring off again enraged, He would remove my husband from that situation. I wasn't going to let that happen. Girl, my husband would not have ever been able to come outside. I would have stalked him for the rest of my life. To avoid that life of humiliation, I have never taken my ring off again that way.

So, we should never go into marriage with divorce as an option. However, God never intended for any of us to be mistreated or abused either. Although He honors the covenant, they can be broken if they are not lining up with His word. I suggest counseling before marriage and divorce.

Now back to what we were initially talking about. What do you do when you are in a loveless marriage? The first thing is you need to examine yourself. We will talk more about self-examination in the next chapter "Fearfully and Wonderfully Made." When self-examining you must figure out what it is that you want. Once you figure that out you then have a foundation to go by. At this time, you can effectively communicate what it is that you want.

I've heard of people sleeping in different bedrooms, and living separate lives, within a marriage. I find that a bit perplexing because marriage is designed to be oneness and not divided. Queen if this is your situation, you have a decision to make.

Now if you are happy this way, too each is its own. However, if you are not happy with this arrangement, you must figure out an approach to either fix it, find a way to live with it, or move on. That last part can be scary. But sometimes that thing that scares us the most is what frees us the best.

Let me make one thing clear I am not condoning divorce. I am pro-marriage. I believe the only way a Christian marriage ends in divorce is because someone in the marriage was not acting Christ-like. They were contrary to the word of God. Anyone who is unfaithful to God has all the traits to be unfaithful to you. I'm not just talking about infidelity. But unfaithful to the vows by not honoring them.

I purposely positioned this chapter closer to the end of the book because we have discussed a lot so far. If this book has blessed you so far, you are equipped with what you need to plan. I know it is not easy to walk away with so many years invested. But was it a good investment? What has your return looked like? Is it an investment you want to retain? Just having a man to call a husband is not what God intended for marriage. Pray about your situation. Find peace. Whatever you do, don't lose yourself. Hold on to you.

To those who are planning to marry, prepare. Please consider counseling. Preferably spiritual counseling. It is imperative you know your mate and all that is attached to him. I know some married women have made marriage look so delightful. Society has made marriage look like a lifeline. The church has marriage look like a requirement to be saved, sanctified, and filled with the Holy Ghost. Our biological clocks make us put marriage on our bucket list. Don't be pressured into it.

A lot of our sisters we see smiling and acting happy are miserable. They are being pretentious to hide what they are feeling. Many of our sisters feel stuck and are truly ashamed of their current situation. If ever exposed to the condition they are living in, it would be embarrassing.

That is why I'm encouraging you to be ready because marriage is work. It takes wisdom for it to survive and thrive.

One of the tools you will need is the ability to ignore. Now I am not talking about ignoring major things like infidelity, addiction, or abuse. I am talking about when they began to act like spoiled brats. Learn to ignore some of the little things that get under your skin. Queen we can not allow everything to take you out of kilter. Child let that man pout. He will be ok. We must learn to pick our battles.

Then there is communication. Again, communication is key. I can't say that enough. If you don't like something, communicate it. A man can't read your mind. Your pouting will not move the meter either sis. Just tell him what you need. Communicating and nagging are not the same. If I ask my husband to fix something and he keeps ignoring it; I will hire someone to do it. I have learned to pick my battles, or I will run myself crazy.

Be spontaneous and spicy. Now I must address something right here. I know none of you are doing this but to those women we know that do it; queens keeping sex from your husband is not biblical nor is it wise. If you are doing that intentionally it's hateful.

How can you punish your "good" man by holding out on him and then expecting him to feel satisfied with you? Queen walk in wisdom. You can't beat the dog and not expect him to bite, eventually.

The word says in James 1:13 that God wouldn't tempt any of us into evil; let's not tempt our husbands into evil. This can go both ways. Men who do this to their wives are out of order as well. Nothing should keep you two from making love except, the intensive care unit, a severe medical condition, or death, point blank and period!

So, ladies let's be more spontaneous. Keeping that spark alive takes creativity. Plan date nights.

Sometimes I will reserve a room at a beautiful hotel for my husband and me, right in the city where we live, just to get away from the same routine at home. I'm trying to keep things spicy.

Marriage can be beautiful. It is the closest relationship to our one with God. It is a sacred covenant, one that God honors.

Marriage is more than guests, a DJ, and cake. It's bigger than a wedding gown and honeymoon. Marriage is a lifetime vow you make with your husband that it's you and him against the world. It's team yall. It's a lifetime commitment and investment. An investment that should render a lifetime of good returns for both of you.

Chapter 16

Fearfully and Wonderfully Made

"If you know your worth you never have to question your

value" ~ R.J. Allen

Do you ever look back at old relationships and say, "what in the entire whole world was I thinking?" Or ever asked yourself, "Why didn't I treat him better? He is a good man." If you've ever asked yourself those questions, congratulations. That my dear is called growth. As we grow and learn to love ourselves more, standards tend to increase as well as our level of accountability.

With growth comes wisdom. With wisdom comes self-examination, self-appraisal, and self-valuation. Self-appraisal (is a time to figure out our strengths and weaknesses) self-examination (areas to improve) self-valuation (determining worth).

When you've overcome a thing and you began to see things more clearly, you can no longer see yourself in situations you once were in. But you must overcome. If you don't overcome, you'll find yourself going through never-ending cycles.

Let's talk about self-examination. Self-examination is when you study your qualities, thoughts, conduct and motives, and introspection. Taking a closer look at the inner man.

During this time, we consider our ways. We consider our hearts, intentions, and motives. Wisdom causes us to question our actions. You see we can't fix ourselves if we are too busy trying to fix others.

Self-examination is important because it gives us a chance to truly look in the mirror. No one is perfect, so there are always areas we can improve in. Examining ourselves allows us to be clear on those things to improve and make a conscious effort to transform those things through a renewed mind.

Remember this is about us and not them. Once we began to take care of ourselves it seems to take blinders off. Things just look different.

Then there is self-appraising. Self-Appraisal is when you are assessing your strengths and weaknesses. The root word in appraise is praise. Therefore, it gives you an opportunity to too your own horn. Self-appraisal encourages finding reasons to be proud of yourself while reflecting on areas that can be strengthened.

In many organizations, there are yearly self-appraisals where the employee reflects on their performance throughout the year.

This is a great self-growth tool used within organizations. The employee gets to set their own long and short-term goals and expectations. The same concept can be applied here.

What are your goals? What are your expectations for every area of your life? What makes you proud of yourself? We need to consider these things. Knowing these things is critical to our growth.

For self-appraisals to be effective we must approach them honestly, critically, and authentically. A self-appraisal will reveal strengths you never knew you had.

Lastly and equally important is self-valuation.

I can't express to you enough how important knowing your worth is. When self-value rises what you will tolerate or settle for in love relationships, or any relationship, for that matter, seems to diminish.

Transparent Moment:

Before self-value took place in me, I settled for the same kind of man. These men were broken, damaged, and insecure. They were true fixer-uppers. By the end of the relationship, I found out I was a fixer-upper too.

They were flawed and so was I.

I picked the man that I believed was down on his luck because it made me feel better about myself. Not better because I had a good heart but better in a superior way.

I was trying to glean some sort of self-valuation through the relationship by dating someone I believed would feel like they were lucky to have the broken me. I figured if they got someone like me, they would hold on to me because I was way out of their class. So, I thought. Sounds familiar? Yes, I am the girl who had a severe case of fixer-upper syndrome. I was happy the day came I was able to re-invent my colors.

This mindset spewed over into my career life, how I raised my children and even my faithfulness to ministry or lack thereof. I didn't think I was worthy of good things. I always thought I had to settle, even on jobs. But not anymore.

Valuation is an estimation of something's worth. In this case your worth. Self-valuation is when you determine what you are worth to yourself.

When it comes to life and love, self-valuation is very important because there are other tentacles attached to self-valuation, like self-esteem and self-respect. If you don't respect yourself, who will?

Queen, you are fearfully and wonderfully made. God designed you with thorough craftsmanship. He was strategic when designing you. He meditated on each blemish, scar, and every hair on your head. Understand just how valuable you are.

Life has a way of stamping a discounted price on us sometimes. Women have always gotten the short end of the stick it seems but like Queen Vashti, we must learn how to walk in our strength. Our main strength is knowing our worth. Because when we know our worth, we never have to question our value.

As we are trying to figure out this love thing let's continue to grow. When we do that, it keeps us ahead of the game.

CHAPTER 17

Queen, It's Your Move

Well, I have come to the end of this book, but I didn't want to close out before reiterating just who you are. What better way to do this than over a game of chess.

In the game of chess, there are several different characters. One of the main pieces in chess is the Queen.

The most important piece in the game is the King. However, the Queen is the strongest. She is the most versatile. She is the key component of the strategies of the game. She can make major moves in all directions. She is one of the most fearsome pieces of the game. She is the only one of her kind on the board. Her main job is to protect her King.

This is you, Queen. You are not replaceable. You are a one-in-a-million. So, if you have your head down shoulders slumped, change your posture. You have no reason to look down.

In the game of chess, it's not wise to send the Queen out with no protection or strategy because of her value. The same applies to you.

Protect your identity by walking in a Queen's behavior. Posture yourself to wholly being dedicated to being whole. Understand in this thing called love there is no need to think like a man. All you should focus on is acting like a lady.

Queen, you can accomplish anything you can dream about so dream big and succeed at something.

When being open to new love relationships have your mental checklist together. Know exactly what you are looking for in a man. Don't settle for fixer-uppers. That relationship can cost you more than it is worth.

As a Queen recognize abuse and bad investments. Don't cast your pearls anywhere.

In the game of chess, the Queen is the only female represented on the board. She proves alone does not mean being lonely.

As the queen strategically waits on the Lord, she understands that she can think outside the box. Who says you can't find love with someone who looks different from you?

When God sends your King don't drag his pearls. Your main job is to protect your King and his pearls.

Neither you nor your King is another person's garbage. You'll just need to learn each other's love language. Queen, it's your job to teach him how to love you.

Queen, you are fearfully and wonderfully made. Once your King has found you use wisdom and speak to the King in him.

Love is a beautiful thing. Because God is love. The first love is self-love. You are unable to love anyone the right way if you neglect loving yourself first.

So, there...Now that you know just how valuable you are I want to enlighten you that in this thing called love, it's chess, not checkers.

Queen, it's your move.

About the Author

Jennifer B. Allen is the founder of Jennifer B. Allen Global Ministries and Lydia's Crown Inc., 501-C3 Non-Profit organization, that seeks to empower women, who have been victims of traumatic events, by offering resources and coaching with a focus on reforming unhealthy mindsets. She is a self-publisher with Reflection Photography and Publishing LLC.

Jennifer B. Allen was raised in the church but strayed away from her upbringing. After years of self-destructive behavior, that consumed her life with drugs and alcohol abuse; her life spiraled out of control. She found herself in and out of mental hospitals, on suicide watch, and almost in prison. When she was tired, Jennifer B. Allen readied herself to allow God to put her back on the Potter's wheel. She said, "Yes" to God and accepted her call as an Evangelist, and was licensed under the leadership of Dr. Crystal Pugh, Global Ministry Center International. She also has the covering of her spiritual mentor Pastor Rosalina Matos, Gospel Light Church, West Palm Beach, FL.

Jennifer B. Allen was accepted into the School of the Great Commission, pursuing her doctoral degree in Christian Counseling. Bestselling Author Jennifer B. Allen has written about her life, which includes the story of her hard-fought battle with breast cancer, and her healing process, in her Amazon Best-Selling book "Hostage in the Mirror." In her book, she describes the steps she took with God; that have led her to experience the life she could only dream about at a time in her life. Jennifer B. Allen has also co-authored several Amazon best-sellers with other great influencers and has independently published in several journals. Jennifer B. Allen is also the host of her daily radio show called "The Inspiration Zone." In her daily show, she spends time on subject matters that affect us all. She brings a daily Jennifer B. Allen Ministries' mission is to help coach God's people through their metamorphosis and healing process. She understands the importance of having a personal relationship with God the Father, Son, and Holy Ghost, to experience life in the

abundance promised to the children of God as
we are fulfilling God's plan for our lives
according to Jeremiah 29:11.

Jennifer B. Allen takes pride in her military
service, serving in the US Marine Corps. She is
a loving wife, a caring and overly protective
mother, a daughter, and a big sister.

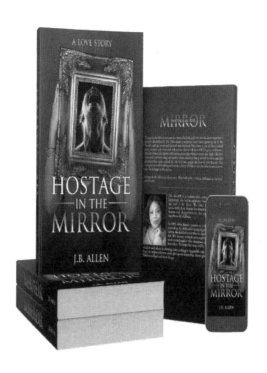

Jenniferballen.com
Facebook: Jennifer B. Allen Ministries
Instagram: Coachj_b_Allen
The Inspiration Zone 1:00 PM Eastern Daily.
WWW.GOSPELTIMEMACHINE.COM

Made in the USA
Columbia, SC
19 September 2022

66972096R00104